Miracle on the Hudson
Survivors Share Their Stories of
Near Death and Hope for New Life

BRACE FOR IMPACT

Dorothy Firman AND Kevin Quirk

Health Communications, Inc.
Deerfield Beach, Florida

www.hcibooks.com

**Library of Congress Cataloging-in-Publication Data
is available through the Library of Congress.**

©2009 Dorothy Firman and Kevin Quirk

ISBN-13: 978-0-7573-1357-8
ISBN-10: 0-7573-3157-4

Publisher: Health Communications, Inc.
   3201 S.W. 15th Street
   Deerfield Beach, FL 33442–8190

Cover design by Larissa Hise Henoch
Interior design and formatting by Dawn Von Strolley Grove

CONTENTS

PREFACE

WHEN I LIVED IN THE HUDSON RIVER VALLEY, I loved taking long walks along the Hudson in all four seasons. I always thought there was something different about that river. Something majestic, something old, something . . . mysterious. That's what I was thinking while I watched one of the evening news magazine shows two days after the Hudson River miracle plane crash on January 15, 2009. Like millions of people everywhere, I had seen the initial reports and needed to see more. The more I saw, the more mesmerized I became.

Then I thought about Charlotte, the planned destination of US Airways Flight 1549. I lived there for seven years while a sports reporter for *The Charlotte Observer,* back when newspapers were still vibrant and Michael Jordan was a college kid. *What must it have been like to be sitting in that plane heading to Charlotte and winding up crashing in the river, then walking away from it,* I wondered. As I learned more details about just how unfathomable this whole near-death experience had been, I felt a stirring. *What just happened here? What did it mean?*

"You have to write a book about this!" my wife, Krista, blurted out.

"I know," I said. "It's the passengers. . . . There's something here, something important."

As a counselor, personal historian, and teacher of memoir-writing classes, I have long been drawn to explore how dramatic life experience can serve as a gateway to a profound new perspective or approach to life. But how would I even find these 150 passengers? What would I say if I *did* find them? How would I earn the trust of people whose lives had just been turned upside down by a combination of terror and jubilation, all about a half-hour apart? How would I explain why I wanted to write such a book, and why on earth they might consider joining me?

Two days later I was making initial phone calls. I tried to find the right words. "I do not mean to disturb you during this traumatic time," I would begin. "It's just that I feel this . . . calling."

And so began my connection with dozens of passengers of Flight 1549. I followed a trail that led me on many twists and turns. When the task of somehow bringing together a sizable group of passengers who hardly knew one another initially appeared too daunting, I worked with one passenger. Then, as they began to bond in cyberspace and in person, I shifted course and reached out to a larger contingent of survivors and first responders.

With the scope of the project expanding, I knew I needed a partner to assist me. That was an easy choice: Dorothy Firman, a friend and colleague who had coauthored three of the *Chicken Soup for the Soul* books. Thankfully, she said yes right away, and she kept saying yes through the many days and weeks when she could have found so many very good reasons to say no. I can't imagine anyone who could have more clearly grasped what this book was about, and what it could be, nor anyone who could smoothly cocreate pivotal decisions while in the midst of a long trip to Russia, Norway,

Finland, and Sweden, presenting on her own books.

Momentum for our book began to gather, then disperse across different paths, then gradually return in a new configuration. All along we held to an idea. All along we have felt honored and deeply appreciative of the connections we have forged with these wonderfully "ordinary" people from Flight 1549.

Now they are here, willing to share who they are and what happened to them, and to try to make some sense out of this celebrated second chance at life. They're here because one way or another they too sense that there's more going on than an uplifting story that captured a public starved for positive news in troubled times.

None of us can know, of course, but we wonder. Not just about the details but the meaning. Could it be that the more we open ourselves to the inspiring lessons and messages this miracle may hold for us, the more our own hearts will be stirred? Could it be that somewhere in those poignant images of passengers standing so peacefully and confidently on the water-covered wings lay the seeds that can help us find the courage, strength, and faith that we as individuals and as a nation need today?

That's what I wanted to explore from that moment two days after the miracle. That's what I am continuing to explore. And that's what we invite you to explore with us.

—*Kevin Quirk*

ACKNOWLEDGMENTS

This has been no ordinary book project and many people came together to make it possible. Our deepest appreciation goes to the twenty-five passengers and first responders from Flight 1549 who have shared their personal stories and their commitment to make a difference in the world. Special thanks to passengers Mark Hood and Don Norton for helping to lay the foundation.

Many thanks to our literary agent, Matthew Carnicelli and the folks at Trident Media Group who recognized the real impact of the Hudson River miracle. At HCI Books, Editorial Director Michele Matrisciani, Web Designer Nicole Haye, Communications Director Kim Weiss, and President Peter Vegso have devoted themselves to books that make a difference. Their faith in this, as an important book, has paved the way.

Kevin appreciates the encouragement from the students of his Fall '09 Writing Your Life Story classes at the University of Virginia School of Continuing and Professional Studies and OLLI, as well as aspiring author Alden Bigelow. Kevin especially extends his gratitude to his wife, Krista Weih, and son, Aibek, for their love, support, and guidance. Krista's ideas were always on target and delivered with compassion for the survivors of Flight 1549 and those who can learn from them.

Dorothy wishes to thank her husband, Ted, who has been there for every one of life's endeavors over more than thirty-five years. And to our children and grandchildren, who are the future. A special thank you to the passengers I interviewed who knew a bit about the story of my critically ill sister and offered, unhesitatingly, their love and support. Thank you, especially, Barry. Your thoughtfulness knows no bounds. To my sister, who is regaining her health, I offer my love. And to my parents, who at ninety years old have spent their lives being good people, I have nothing but gratitude.

Part I
Beyond the Hudson

I am not afraid of tomorrow, for I have seen yesterday and I love today.

—William Allen White

1
The *Real* Impact

All of life is a near-death experience.

—Alan Harris

"Brace for impact." We all remember those three chilling words. We tried to imagine how we would have reacted as that plane plunged toward the Hudson. Would we have prayed? Screamed? Locked arms with the stranger beside us? Reached for our cell phones to leave a final message with those we love? Stared out the windows to glimpse how the disaster would play out—or for any sign of hope?

We all know what happened next. Sully's astounding landing. Passengers clinging to one another on those partially submerged wings. Ferries and rescue boats rushing in as if on cue from a Hollywood director. Every single person getting out alive, with nothing worse than soggy clothes and mostly minor injuries. We shook our heads, clutched our hands, praised God, or just watched in awe. How did that happen? What could it mean? We watched and read all about this stunning tale of survival against all odds.

Now it's time for a different, perhaps more meaningful story. What happened to these 150 passengers when they went *home*? What was it like to return to their families, their homes, their jobs—everything that was familiar but some-how not the same? How did they celebrate coming back from the brink? How did they confront the near-death trauma? How did their loved ones respond to the miracle in the house? What has been the *real* impact they braced for, not of the disaster they expected, but of the gift of a "new" life?

That's what you're about to discover. As we go forward you will visit with many of those passengers, along with first responders and others involved in the crash and rescue that touched us all. These ordinary people who lived an extraor-dinary experience will be opening their hearts, minds, and souls to share their honest accounts of the unfolding of their lives after Flight 1549 became firmly imprinted on their per-sonal history and our cultural landscape.

Their stories of finding meaning and hope will speak to questions you may have:

- How has the miracle changed how they relate to their husbands, wives, children, and other loved ones?
- How has it impacted how they perceive God, or the world around them?
- What do they most remember when they think back to that day on the Hudson, or do they try not to think about it at all?
- How do they feel when they get on a plane today, or have they sworn off air travel forever?
- Do they ever ask "Why me?" If they do, what answer comes back?

As you read their stories, in their own words, you will learn that some passengers have already taken courageous steps toward new goals and visions, while others explore possibilities they may never have dreamed of before the Hudson.

For others, the changes may look not so dramatically different on the *outside* but feel markedly new on the *inside*. These subtle but profound differences are about love, about healing, about hope. The changes may have to do with a shift in perspective on what matters and what doesn't. It may be a yearning for a change they want to see reflected in life around them, and what they can do to make it happen. Some feel so full of compassion and gratitude they hardly know what to do with it!

Some survivors of Flight 1549 are finding that life beyond the Hudson is much more about coming home to what they already knew. But even in that reclaiming, something feels different—there's a deeper respect, understanding, or appreciation for familiar beliefs or values. They may sit down to Thanksgiving dinner at the same table with the same people, but what they see and feel may be entirely new.

Other passengers and first responders are not looking for neon light answers or bumper sticker revelations. Instead, they find themselves asking a whole lot more questions, and it's the asking that has reconfigured their lives. Isn't that the way it often works? You're hit with some unexpected crisis or challenge, and when you get through it, your head is full of questions about what happened and what to make of it. Some questions may be disturbing, at least initially, while others are soothing or uplifting. Ultimately, all have the capacity to help you grow. And often that's just what happens. Growth, change, even transformation.

In her bestselling book *Broken Open: How Difficult Times Can Help Us Grow*, Elizabeth Lesser suggests that what most shakes us up also carries the inherent capacity to enrich us. We can, she suggests, be the phoenix rising from the ashes. And make no mistake: contrary to any myth that all those passengers of Flight 1549 left that sinking airliner with a carefree grin, this stunning near-death moment shook almost everyone in that cabin to the core. Now they're slowly coming back to "life"—growing, changing, and rearranging how they relate to their faith, to others, to the world. They are riding the waves of one big, public, broken-open experience.

They're also learning that you don't survive a plane crash and find yourself all put neatly back together right away. That's natural. It takes time after the shake-up to discover who you are, or who you want to be. Through their stories, the passengers are sharing this second chance at life as it evolves, and we get to be right there in the middle of it with them.

You may be reading this book simply because you were touched by the event and are curious about what happened to the passengers after their worst nightmare turned into their greatest gift. Your curiosity certainly will be answered. But you will find that in reading these stories and reflections, you will gain something more: ideas, lessons, inspirations that come from that deep place inside few of us are prompted to visit. The people you are about to get to know have been to that place. Most are still in it. Their stories of hope and faith born from the winds of a crisis and the dawn of an awakening may comfort, guide, or inspire you in your own life. You may ask yourself: how would it change my life if that happened to *me*?

Maybe you're in the midst of your own trauma or shakeup: an accident or major illness in your life or in your family; the loss of a job or fear of losing one; those anxieties about money or love or an uncertain future that can weigh us down. If you're not in a crisis or challenge today, these stories may provide insight and understanding about hardships you have encountered and survived. And even if you're not wrestling with difficult times, this book will offer timely reminders that all of us, at any time or phase of life, have access to greater purpose and meaning. What these twenty-five passengers and first responders share will stir your own ideas about the importance of family, knowing what really matters, living with more gratitude, finding our courage, respecting our fears, discovering our purpose, and recognizing how something good really can emerge out of crisis and tragedy.

Chances are, you will find commonality with many of these contributors. You will hear from Lucille, an eighty-five-year-old woman hardly able to walk, who, after the plane splashed down in the Hudson with her daughter Diane sitting next to her, was prepared to make one final, dramatic, motherly sacrifice. You will get to know Bill and Michele, two twenty-somethings who would rather never fly again, and business executives and sales managers who must fly all the time. You will meet Maryann, who survived several near-tragedies before the crash, and Debbie, who had to confront a new and unexpected crisis weeks after the crash. You will visit with Darren and Don, two coworkers who became "brothers" after surviving Flight 1549 together, and Glenn, who has helped build a vibrant community among the 150 former strangers who share this new bond.

You will hear from parents who believed they would never see their teenagers, toddlers, or a child on the way. You will meet an ex-Marine officer, a swimming pool serviceman, a nurse, a TV executive, a CEO, and a boat pilot. You will learn about the experiences of many survivors who have publicly spoken about their experience at churches, schools, businesses, and organizations as large as the American Red Cross, as well as those who remain private. You will witness sadness and fear, but you will also notice humor, thoughtfulness, inspiration, and hope.

In some stories, you will read passionate expressions related to religion and faith. Many passengers are devout Christians, others practice different faiths, some regard themselves as spiritual people with no link to any religion, and a few hold more personal views. Because faith is indelibly linked to the experience and perspective of many passengers, each contributor was encouraged, if they chose, to freely share the spiritual dimensions of their story from their own lens to make their accounts richer, deeper, and more personal.

We usually don't get to choose who comes along with us on our "plane crash." We just hope that when trouble hits, we can somehow find the love, support, and guidance to get through it, and, ideally, come out stronger, wiser, more engaged with life. That's how it's worked for the survivors of Flight 1549. They made it, with lots and lots of help. They have reached the other side. And they have emerged with something more, something we all seek. Some spark of hope, some strong pull forward, some sense that there's more going on around us than we can even imagine.

On January 15, 2009, we were all touched by what happened on the Hudson River. We all felt the awe of a moment spiraling toward doom transformed into the gift of survival. Now, through the words and feelings of those who were there, we have an opportunity to be moved by the *meaning* behind the miracle, not just in that one moment but in the ensuing weeks and months, in all our days. In these times of uncertainty, we can stop and remember: We are all survivors. We can all be touched by grace.

2

AWAKENING TO PURPOSE:
Lessons for Us All

The purpose of life is a life of purpose.

—Robert Byrne

EVERYONE IS LOOKING FOR A GOOD LIFE, from the kid on the playground to the rich and famous. And everyone in between. Poets, philosophers, and religious leaders all offer wisdom to guide us toward that good life. Scientists and psychologists study it, looking for everything from the cure to the common cold to how to be happy. And each of us—mother, father, sister, brother, daughter, and son—looks upon our own lives with that question in mind.

What is a good life . . . for me? Because of course it will be different for each of us. And it is never a simple formula, though we often confuse ourselves with the idea that it is. "If only I had _____ [fill in the blank], then I'd be happy." Win the lottery, get a good job, have kids, find the perfect mate, lose weight, be blond, do something great. The list goes on. But happiness defined more broadly is about meaning, about well-being and contentment. Figuring out what this means, for you or me, is a life's work, a process. We don't arrive at a good life, then live in it. We create and recreate and create again a good life over a lifetime. This is the work of the soul, the process of awakening to our purpose. When we are awake to our own unique life purpose, our preferences, our common annoyances or desires, all fade in light of the deep knowing of what is purposeful.

Each of the people involved in this book—passengers, first responders, and authors—have come face-to-face with issues of life purpose. What is important to me? Am I living a life that carries my deepest values? Am I awake to purpose? Each of our passengers was thrust into asking that question, and each has risen to the occasion to answer it.

So what can we learn now from the stories of passengers, first responders, and others connected to Flight 1549? After all, these are average people, on an average day, going about their business, without any intention to be teachers and guides for the rest of us. Men and women going on vacation, going home, traveling for business, on a rescheduled flight, on the plane they often take. People like you and me.

And yet, as each of these people faced the loss of not only a good and meaningful life but of any life at all, they have had to dig deep to recast their lives around meaning and purpose and values. They have found themselves working harder to find the core of what makes a life good, for them. They have had to find and renew their faith. They have had to remember and recommit to the importance of their families and communities. They have had to honor and bring forth their strengths and talents and the deepest qualities of their souls.

Our travelers (passengers, first responders, friends and family, witnesses) have been passionately engaged in this search for purpose. They have been following the path of heart in finding their own good life, and, as we travel with them, we will learn from them and find ourselves a bit closer to our own good life.

Before we visit with those remarkable people, let's visit some of the key qualities that they have taken ownership of as they came back from the brink of death and renewed or reshaped their quest for a good life. Awakening to purpose is about awakening to the qualities of our own being and living in congruence with those qualities. There are many qualities that each of us may nurture in ourselves. There is no definitive list, no set of qualities we *should* have. But as we visit these survivors, we will see some common themes, shared qualities that they have . . . and that we have as well. Each of us can open the door that allows us to nurture these qualities in ourselves and in our world.

Faith

Faith, as we know, is not something that we do just on Sundays, just at church, just through our religion or prayers. Faith defines a life. Many of our travelers lead their whole lives based in and living through their faith. Faith sustained many, if not most of the passengers on Flight 1549 during the crash landing, in those minutes where death seemed inevitable, and in the miraculous days, weeks, and months that followed. Faith, of course, is larger than any one religion and is, in fact, not bound by any religious orientation. Faith is so much larger, that everyone is invited, at all times, to find it. Faith in God, in the universe, in our fellow beings, in ourselves. Faith in those we love and faith that we can find a way to be true to ourselves, even in hard times. Faith in reflection, prayer, meditation, and an inner orientation, and faith manifest in expression, in giving, and in outer action. And this large faith invites us into many more qualities, each one part of the path to purpose.

Gratitude

Gratitude is a natural happiness at getting something we want, a social convention designed to create a more civilized world and a spiritual truth with the potential to change lives. Whether in children or adults, the simple expression of gratitude uplifts the spirits of giver and receiver. And yet, especially in difficult times, and these *are* difficult times, it is often our default pattern to notice what we don't have, what we want and aren't getting. We can drag ourselves down in ideas of what life *should* be like. And most of us spend way too much time with a cast of inner voices and negating messages about how *we* should be.

Through each of their stories, our travelers will help remind us of the importance of gratitude, for the biggest miracles and the smallest moments. Gratitude at being alive to meet your new baby: there's a miracle to be thankful for!

Gratitude for mowing the lawn on a hot, humid day? *Yes!* That too.

Whenever our lives evolve in a way that feels meaningful and important, whether it's in a moment or over a long period, gratitude arises in us. That's happened in a big way for these passengers and those close to them. They remind us that while gratitude thrives in good times, its real gift comes to us in hard times. To find gratitude in the midst of hardship, loss, fear, and doubt is to claim the deepest gratitude that human beings have: gratitude for this very life, just as it is, in this moment. As you meet each of these people, you will find that they have learned this lesson, and they invite us, by their very lives, to learn it as well.

Love

Love is the holding environment in which souls are nourished. It is in the experience of love, giving, and receiving that we have the potential to grow to be our best. Love, however, comes in many flavors and with as many subtle tones as a great piece of music. It ranges from a first crush, to the gentle fondness we feel for a friend, to the passion of true love, and on to the experience of worship that comes as an expression of a love of God. It can be known in playfulness, and it can be serious and thoughtful. It is unique in each relationship and a common bond we all share.

In the stories that follow, we will see love in all its many aspects through the eyes of people who thought they might lose it. Folks young and old, passengers and rescuers, family and friends—all awakened to how much love they felt. "Last" phone calls expressed love to family members who didn't yet know what had happened. Strangers on lifeboats felt love for people they would never see again.

Luckily, love is not something we have to study. It is something we are. When we peel back the layers, or in profound moments like this experience, we find ourselves as people who love. We love others in their humanness, which means we love them with all their faults and imperfections. And that, too, is a lesson we learn from passengers who, facing the loss of those they loved, learned to love them all the more and accept them all the more fully.

But love is not just an inner experience. It is also expression, behavior, and action. Risking yourself to save another in a crisis is an act of love. Saying "I love you" is, too. Our travelers from the Hudson have come to see just how important it is to say "I love you" in words and in deeds. Whether it is a hug (or a hugger), or service to the world, expressing love is what our passengers are teaching us to do. Not just once, at a crisis time, and not just as a ritual, on the way out the door, but over and over again, throughout a lifetime.

Wisdom

If love stirs the heart, wisdom stirs the mind. And we need both for a good life. It is in our wisdom that we know what is right for us, what is true, what makes sense. Allowing ourselves to claim our own wisdom and to build wisdom over a lifetime will strengthen our character, build in us confidence and capacity. Whether our wisdom in any moment is common wisdom or spiritual wisdom, it is our North Star, the guiding light that helps us find the way.

When your plane is going down, it helps to have a little wisdom to fall back on. You may be the passenger who has read the safety card or looked for the nearest exit. That's some good, down-to-earth wisdom. You may be the passenger who feels held by God or the Universe, and at peace. That is the really big wisdom that we all aspire to and that we all know, some of the time.

Our travelers were thrown into a life-and-death situation out of which a wider vision emerged. They found wisdom in the moment of danger and they built on that foundation to go on to live wiser lives. When the stakes are that high, priorities change. But we needn't wait for that kind of crisis to become wise. All it takes, really, is remembering what our highest values are, where our priorities lie, who we deeply are and want to be.

Healing

From the depths of faith, through gratitude, love, and wisdom, each of us, as travelers on the path of life, requires healing. Life is often hard, unfair. We are wounded by accident, by omission, by fate. Sometimes we are wounded by those we love and sometimes by the world at large. The plane crash, the war, the loss of a loved one, the injury or illness, the childhood trauma—all set the stage for our need to heal. And what a magnificent piece of work healing is. Just watching the x-rays of a child's arm, first broken and then healed, tells us how healing happens . . . slowly but surely over weeks or months, with good attention paid to the wound and healing energy brought to bear. For the broken arm, we need a cast. For loss, we need grief. For trauma, we need time.

For our passengers, the journey of healing was launched by a moment of facing almost certain death. For most of us, the injury is usually less dramatic. But there will be things in common on all healing journeys. Among them is that healing is a total experience in which mind, body, emotions, and spirit all renew themselves. And, as they say, time heals all wounds. So patience is required. Many of the survivors of Flight 1549 are practicing patience. For some, the injury of this near-death experience seemed slight. For others, it was huge. But for each person, through the passing of time, through silence, through help, through prayer, through service to others, through telling their stories and living their lives, healing is happening.

In the end, healing is no more than the process of life and no less than our greatest achievement. Some of the stories you are about to read will illustrate that in profound ways. Healing is a gift we give to ourselves, first by knowing that we are hurt and second by honoring ourselves enough to heal consciously. It is all too easy to look away from what hurts and put on a good show of being okay. Sometimes we have no choice but to do that. However, the richer life will emerge from a thoughtful consideration of our own wounds, our own needs, and our own path of healing. The person we become as we heal will be all that we were before and more. Our passengers are a testimony to that truth.

Transformation

We have seen miracles and we have seen hard work. We understand, through our travelers, that life itself is a miracle. They learned this the hard way. We walk slowly but surely up the mountain, and suddenly a gust of wind, a bird, or an angel helps us up the steepest slope. And then we walk again. We experience our faith, and then it goes behind a cloud. Our love gets lost in anger . . . for a moment. Gratitude struggles against bitterness and wisdom battles ignorance. This is the way of life. No one travels a straight and narrow path from birth to death. It is a long and winding road, and on it we meet everyone and everything. Transformation is available at every turn in the road. It is the process of learning what life has to teach us and healing ourselves of all that has hurt us.

Transformation is visible all the time: the bud of a new flower, the sun rising in the east, a child's first steps. Magic! The plane that lands in the Hudson, the lives that are saved, the hard work that follows for each and every passenger— transformation! We are all transformed by joy and beauty, by the glory in the world and the spirit of God. This is the magic and the mystery. The gift that is given. This is the miracle. And right next to every miracle is a piece of work that needs to be done. We never have one without the other.

All of us, living in this moment, are invited to open our hearts to the miracles that come our way. Some will be huge, as this flight on January 15, 2009, was. Some will be tiny: a synchronicity we experience, a sudden insight, a moment of noticing, an unexpected smile. Allowing the presence of these miracles is allowing ourselves to partake of the breath of life. But when we have been given a miracle, it is required that we do something with it. This is what our passengers teach us. When we take in a breath of air, we must breathe out. And transformation is the process that comes through breathing in and breathing out. Oxygen feeds our bodies, creating all of the miraculous effects of life. Carbon dioxide is released, feeding the world outside and eliminating the toxins within.

The miracle given is followed by the hard work of integrating whatever new learning has come our way. A miracle that we keep to ourselves is perhaps no miracle at all. A lesson learned, but not shared, is not well learned. A gift received, when none is given back, is empty. The travelers from Flight 1549 can serve to remind us at every turn that life is a miracle, that there is a time and place to learn and to heal, and that sharing the gifts we are given is one of the most profound ways of awakening to purpose.

Part II
Life Is a Miracle

There are only two ways to live your life. One is as though nothing is a miracle. The other is as though everything is a miracle.

—Albert Einstein

3
Barry Leonard:
HEART OF GRATITUDE

It is better to give than to receive.

In Barry's Fifth Avenue office, I am greeted warmly by everyone, from the doorman to the receptionist to Barry himself. It is clear, before I even meet Barry Leonard, that the people around him care deeply for him. After the crash and the week's recuperation (pretty much forced on him by friends and doctors). Barry was ready to get back to work. Commuting every week from Charlotte to New York, he did so again, "ready to put this accident behind me." When he stepped off the elevator (sixth floor) there was a huge poster, with notes and pictures and signatures of his many employees, coworkers, and friends. Barry was moved, close to tears, but more deeply, he was moved closer again to his deep appreciation of all the people he cares about, all who have helped him, all those he loves, all those whose lives he has been touched by. His office staff also gave him a plaque with a picture of Lou Gehrig and the famous words he said when diagnosed with a debilitating and ultimately fatal illness, how he considered himself "the luckiest man on the face of the earth."

Barry thinks of himself that way, as one of the luckiest men alive. Barry, as a CEO and businessman at the top of his field, is really, in the end, a people person. His business successes can be attributed to many things, most notably hard work, strong will, and a clear eye on the prize. But more than all of this, I believe, Barry is where he is and who he is because he cares. It's easy for Barry to note who has helped him and given to him, and harder for him to acknowledge his own role as a good man. I push him from time to time to find out more. "You have a lot of heroes," I say. "Who are you a hero to?" Barry is slow to respond to this particular question, but over our time together, I find out about a few of the people he has touched.

"I was a taker for thirty-five years, but now I give back," he said. I think he was always a giver. It just took time for Barry to notice it. This accident has rocked the boat for Barry, as it has for so many, but it has sent him back, more deeply, into core values: values honed over a lifetime. While I was talking to him, he excused himself to take a call on his cell phone. It was his daughter, flying home. "I love you," he said as he ended the call. Apologizing to me for our interruption, I reminded him that he was keeping his values straight right then and there. His daughter was more important. Funny, when I canceled our first meeting because my sister was in the hospital, he said the exact same thing to me: "Your sister is more important." And weeks later when we met, he re-membered my sister in the hospital and asked how she was.

By the time I leave his office several hours later, we have

*laughed together, shed a few tears, and talked about what
is really important. We talked about family and heroes,
about work ethic and gratitude, about giving and receiving. I am touched by this good man. As I get up to leave, we
start to shake hands, but quickly it becomes a hug.*

—Dorothy

In Barry's Words

I KNEW IT WAS GOING TO BE A COLD, snowy day on January 15.
Funny thing: I'd changed the dress policy in my New York
company a few years ago. Jeans were now okay. That was a
new idea for me, but folks loved it. Me, I never once wore
jeans, until that day. But the weather was nasty. I was walking
through the city a lot on my way to the airport, so I put them
on instead of my usual suit. Employees who saw me that day
started clapping. "You've finally joined the twenty-first
century!" I've never worn them to work again. Don't think I
ever will.

I knew the plane would be late. I'm known as a road war-
rior, since I take over one hundred flights a year. Boarding, I
recognized the captain and some of the crew. I was a regular
on this flight. So were they. At 3:26 the wheels were up and
ninety seconds later, we were traveling at 250 miles per hour
at an altitude of 3,000 feet. The plane shuddered. There was
the smell of fire. There was little talking throughout the
plane. My seatmate, Paul, said it looked like the engine was

going to fall off. Since I was sitting in an aisle seat and not thinking clearly, I undid my seat belt and stepped to the window to look out. "I've got good news and bad news," I said to him. "The engine is not falling off, but it's not running either!" None of us really knew that we'd lost both engines. I knew we were in trouble, though. The plane banked sharp left and felt like a roller coaster as we headed down at an incredibly fast pace. We cleared the George Washington Bridge by 900 feet. It was 3:29! Right about then, the captain made his first and only announcement. "This is the captain. Brace for impact!" Having put my seat belt back on, I put my head down as instructed. I heard later that air traffic thought he was kidding when he told them "We'll be in the Hudson." I don't think Sully kids about things like that.

All I could think about was my conversation with God the day before. My wife was getting test results back for the possibility of breast cancer. I was at work while we were waiting for the results. I had a hard time waiting to hear. I went into my office and closed my door. *God, please let my wife be okay. If you are going to take someone, please take me.* When she called to say she was okay, I wept. Now, as the plane went down, I was facing my death, the death I had offered to God in exchange for my wife. I smiled to myself: *I guess I'm going to get what I asked for.* I was totally at peace. When Larry King asked me about that experience of peace, just a few days after the crash, I wasn't ready to share my private story with anyone. Now I am.

I could see the Manhattan skyline as we went down. Paul

grabbed my arm, drawing me back from my internal world. "We're going to die, aren't we?" he asked. When we hit, at 150 miles per hour, the impact was horrific as the plane slowed in seconds to a complete stop, groaning as it did. It was 3:31! Unbeknownst to me at the time, I had broken my sternum on impact. I looked out the window, and all I could see was water. I thought we had gone under. Very quickly I could see light and buildings as the spray washed down the sides of the plane. Captain Sullenberger came out of the cockpit and yelled "Evacuate!" As I got up and started to move I looked back at my seat to see if my body was still there. The scene from *Ghost* where Patrick Swayze sees his own body came right into my mind. I had yet to have any experience of real fear of dying, but I was glad to see that my body was still with me.

The raft at our exit didn't inflate and the attendant yelled "Jump! Jump! Jump!" And I did . . . into the Hudson, thirty-six degrees. This was the first time I was worried. I knew I'd last about five minutes in the water. With water that cold, hypothermia sets in fast. Later I found out that I could have experienced sudden cardiac arrest or cold shock syndrome. Either could have killed me. I could see the Manhattan shore and realized that I could not make it there. So, I swam toward the front of the plane so that I could see where the New Jersey shore was. For all I knew, we were fifty yards from shore. When I realized we were in the middle of the Hudson River, I swam back where I had come from hoping to get on the fuselage and wing. I saw that the raft was now deployed! What a beautiful sight! I swam toward the raft. To this day, I have no idea how I got into the raft. I had been in the water for over three minutes and believe that I was starting to lose my cognitive abilities. But coming out of the water, soaking wet and shaking uncontrollably, I heard a voice say, "Sir, you have to get out of those clothes now or you are going to freeze to death." I took off my shirt and undershirt even though the wind chill factor was eleven degrees. Derek Alter, who was a pilot traveling back to Charlotte, took off his pilot's shirt and helped me put it on. He put his arm around me and told me to do the same and said that he would keep me warm until help came. He was one of the angels that helped save my life!

When a ferry came near, we asked for a knife to cut us free, so we wouldn't go down with the plane. Cold as I was, I felt myself part of a group effort. I heard Captain Sullenberger, who was in my raft say, "Let the injured, women, and children go first." I remember a girl who was gray and despondent and couldn't get up the ladder to the ferry. I pushed with all my remaining strength and someone from above pulled. She made it. And so did I.

I was in bad shape, though I didn't realize it. Doctor Hilda Roque-Dieguez, the doctor who was at the site of the rescue, told me later that I was lying on the floor when she first got to me. I have no memory of that time. She worried that I'd nicked my heart when my sternum was broken. My blood pressure was high; I was close to having a stroke. They rushed me by ambulance to the hospital and in the ER, I heard them say, "four milligrams morphine." That caused me my second round of worry. *Something must be wrong if they're doing that.* The last real fear? Seeing a chaplain outside of my room, talking to a nurse. *Uh-oh, what does that mean?*

Seeing Hilda [whose story will appear later] and the hospital staff six months later at a gratitude luncheon I co-hosted with Dave Sanderson at Palisades Medical Center, and going back to those rooms, saying thank-you and hugging every person who was there for me, has brought me full circle. From being at death's door to feeling my heart open as I expressed my gratitude, this was big for me. How often do we get to go back to where something bad happened and make it all right? I think it meant a lot to them, too. Dr. Roque-Dieguez was another of my angels! I didn't know it at the time, but she came to the scene, uncalled. She looked to the care of everyone, she found me—in bad trouble—and moved the system along so quickly that I was hospitalized (and saved) within minutes. She told a reporter at the luncheon, "This is the greatest gift a doctor can receive. I'm just happy." What could be better than being able to give back a little bit?

I knew, even in high school, that my life's work was to leave this world a better place than I found it. If I think back to my childhood, I always had visions for a better life, a better world. One of my heroes was Mighty Mouse . . . "Here I come to save the day." He was just a little guy doing great things. But I also loved Elvis Presley and that was about passion. And daring to be different. Being someone who helps and being someone with passion—those two values have really defined the purpose of my life.

There are a lot of people who have helped me to be where I am today, to be who I am. I can't list them all. It starts with my family, of course. My mom always said to me, "You know, Barry, you can go anywhere with an education." I believed her and worked hard in high school. I wasn't the brightest kid in school, by any means, but even then, I worked hard every day. If I got one B my dad would say, "Why the B?" It was his way of pushing me to be the best I could be. His tough style didn't work as well for my brother. He struggled more than I did. But my dad also said, "If you don't have something good to say, don't say anything." And I believed him on that one. And my grandparents, they were models for me, too. Good folks. My grandfather had a philosophy that was pretty simple: Be happy all the time! I can still hear his laugh. He danced at his one-hundredth birthday party. That was a sight. And he smiled . . . and so do I. Most times you'll see me with a smile. But I got my deepest values from the women: my mom and grandmother. Dad died twenty years ago, but my mother is still going strong. She has always been there for me.

In 1977 after I finished graduate school and before my work life began, I saw my brother was in trouble. His life wasn't working out very well. I said to him, "Come on, I'm going to take you to Europe!" I wanted to inspire him. I knew that passion was key to getting anywhere in life, and he didn't have it then. I told the folks who offered me a job straight out of grad school, "Sorry, I can't start 'til the fall." I also didn't have money. My family wasn't wealthy, I'd been in school, working to pay for it, but I had to do this. I took out a loan. I paid back

$179.63 every month for four years to make that trip happen. It was the best thing I ever did! My brother went on to college, and he's been doing really well ever since.

So many people have gone out of their way to help me, just as I tired to help my brother. My mentor in business, Pete Scotese, said to me early on, "Barry, when you die, you'll be remembered either as a giver or a taker. Which do you want to be?" I've never forgotten that, and he's still my friend and mentor at eighty-nine years old, and now I get to give back some to him, as well. I stay connected to folks from throughout my life because this is something that is really important to me. It's why I had to reconnect with Hilda and Derek. If someone is important to me, I want to keep them in my life, and if I'm important to them, I hope they keep connected to me as well. I have so many close friends, from high school on. And so many have been good to me.

At the hospital, after the accident, they sent someone in and asked if I'd like help talking about the accident. I said yes. This is when I realized I needed help. But I was holding it all in for the first week, and then one day, by the fire with my wife, it just opened up and I felt the feelings: fear, loss, sadness, grief. During the actual accident I went into Marine mode. I'm strong, but even in my weakened state on the raft I was doing what I could to help others. There was no way I was going to let anyone struggle without giving a helping hand. My own need for help came later, first at the rescue site and later when I knew I needed emotional and spiritual help. It took me a while to realize I even needed it.

You know, Dave Sanderson [whose story will appear later] has asked me to speak with him about the accident. I love that guy. He realized that his therapy was speaking to others and inspiring them. But we're so different. I've done big things with companies, turning them around, pulling things together, making an impact, and one time failing to save a company. I don't see myself as a public speaker, but I admire this God-given talent in Dave. I said no to Dave for a long time but did make a short speech at our thank-you luncheon and then made my first and last real speech to a church in Goldsboro, where one of my companies is. I wrote that speech out and my wife said, "Barry, you won't be able to do this." She knows how emotional I am. I knew she was right, but I did it anyway, stopping to cry when I needed to.

I've always been emotional, but only in private. Now I'm willing to let it out. I'm okay with that part of me. This is one thing that's really changed. My heart flies open so much, and I get a little choked up. I don't care. That doesn't bother me. If that happened before the accident, I'd be a wreck, not maintaining my "image." Now I'm true to myself, true to my feelings. After the speech a World War II vet came up to me to tell me about his experience landing on Normandy beach. He told me, "I know what you went through." And he started to weep. So did I. We left each other with a hug. A man I've never met, but a kindred spirit for sure.

About ten years ago, my son got hit in the head by a baseball. We didn't know at first how bad it was, but in the end it was a life-or-death experience. Epidural hematoma, emergency brain surgery. We didn't know if he'd make it or be damaged in some way. I'm not an overly religious man, but that was God talking to me, saying, "Listen to me!" I listened, first just thinking it was about my son. We were home after the accident, and I was checking on him every hour. Waking myself up to check. When he said, "Daddy, I have a headache" I rushed him to the hospital. But it was more than that. Watching someone I love face death, I took stock of my life and realized I didn't want to keep doing life the way I was. At that time I was working all the time for a company, moving to get ahead. My wife said, "Honey, you've always wanted to run your own business, so go do it!" And I did, nine months after my son's accident. I learned a lot, but the business failed! When I got hired to become Chief Executive Officer of Excell Home Fashions, they said to me, "It's not for your twenty years of success that we hired you. It's for the two years of being with a company that went under. You've been through the fire!" The fire is about the passion. No one is always just a winner. But the passion keeps us going, even during hard times.

Now I wonder what this recent accident has to teach me. It's been a rough year, with a few other health scares, two of which resulted in surgery. I've lost some things that were important to me. I can't run anymore. I've run the New York Marathon and many other races over the years, but now I have to exercise more carefully. So many events have made me think about my mortality. I find myself praying every day, sometimes for myself, mostly for others. Two of my Chinese friends,

Wellington Pan and Wang Mei, told me that out of these dangerous situations comes a long life! I hope they are right. And an old high school friend said, "Everything in life averages out." I've had good and bad. Everyone has. But it all comes back to leaving the world a better place, the thing I figured out in high school, though I don't really know how I did that!

I just got a call from a young kid in North Carolina. You talk about meaning, purpose, and values. More than anything, giving does it. He said to me, "Mr. Leonard, I can't thank you enough. I got in! I'm going to school." I help kids go to college who couldn't otherwise. They have to do the work and they have to have passion, but I do my part by making it possible financially. Every year I help a few and it makes life much sweeter.

There are so many givers . . . of time and money and . . . spirit, I guess. So many people I have to be thankful for. And I guess some whom I've helped, too. I've had family and mentors and my wife, and friends and colleagues who've given me so much. I have my best buddies from way back. I've just been honored in the business world with an award. I was so humbled that my colleagues thought I was of this much value. I called my wife . . . and my mom to share the news with them. I'm proud of myself. That's okay to say now. I don't think I could have said that before the accident. I think I'm changed, a better man, a kinder man.

Recently, we had to lay people off in one of my businesses. Times are hard economically. Most people understand about me that I'm an openhearted guy, but I'm also a businessman.

I had to lay off one gentleman. He came into my office and just sat there, in shock. He told me his wife had cancer. I said, "We'll find you a job, John." I couldn't lay him off. This is the first time in my career that I backed away from a good business decision. But laying this man off, at such a difficult time in his life, wasn't a good humanitarian decision, and that is more important. I know that now. When he left, we hugged. I myself had sat where he sat, wondering about my wife's life, going down in a plane to what could have been my death. How could a good business decision outweigh caring for a fellow human being?

I was on a flight just a few days ago with two other passengers from 1549. That's not unusual. Many of us fly these same flights weekly. I looked back to see that Denise was crying. Another passenger, Steve, was holding her hand. It never occurred to me not to reach out. I reached back across the aisle and held her other hand. Many of us still have a hard time with flights. I only want to reach out and share, and if it's someone else crying or me crying, I want to be there for that. I'm okay with me now. Old self-doubt and criticism, trying too hard, needing to look good, getting caught in superficial things—that's all changed, pretty drastically. I'm not trying to be anybody else. Be the best me I can. Be Barry.

P.S. The healing has continued for Barry in the months since we met. Therapy has helped him to deal with a recurring nightmare of walking across a frozen river (Hudson?) and falling in just fifty yards from shore. Then, on October

1, acting on a tip, he was able to make a reservation for the celebrated reunion flight from LaGuardia to Charlotte piloted by Sully Sullenberger and copilot Jeff Skiles. He even got his same seat, 1C. Before the flight, he shook hands with Sully. "Barry, it's great to see you again, and we will take care of you," Sully said.

"It was one of the smoothest flights I have ever been on," Barry said afterward. "This was my seventy-fifth flight since January 15. The first seventy-four were full of anxiety and apprehension, but I felt only elation and security on this flight. This is part of my healing process. It was important for me to complete the circle. I hope that all of my future flights will be as easy as this one."

I hope so, too. Barry is heading off to India and China within the next few days, the longest flight he will have taken since the miracle landing.

—Dorothy

4
Bill Elkin:
WHY AM I HERE?

*There are two great days in a person's life—the
day we are born and the day we discover why.*

—William Barclay

*It's a warm June afternoon, and as we meet over coffee
near his home in Mooresville, North Carolina, Bill Elkin
tells me that he is eagerly anticipating Father's Day. He will
be speaking to a group of dads and sons at a church dinner.
He plans to talk about the importance of making connections and keeping them alive, about being honest and especially about shaking stereotypes. "Boys need different role
models today," he says. "You don't have to practice tough
love. And as a son, it's okay to have feelings and show
them." Bill does not have a son of his own. He has long been
estranged from his own father, who left his family when Bill
was young. Yet it is very clear in getting to know Bill that
he has much to offer those fathers and sons. With his
daughters, Katie and Lily, his priorities are clear: family
time really matters.*

I've also learned that Bill is a thoughtful, caring, deeply feeling man. Like many male survivors of Flight 1549, he has allowed himself to dive fully into the emotions spurred by the crash. He isn't running from them or keeping them at bay in the name of "staying strong." Strength, he is learning, can actually come from a willingness to be vulnerable. It's a tough lesson for any man in our culture to grasp, but Bill doesn't fear it.

Neither is Bill shying away from asking the big questions about what the Miracle on the Hudson means. They are the same questions we all ask: Why are we here? What is our purpose, our calling? What are we meant to do with this great gift of life? For many of the survivors of Flight 1549, those questions have echoed through almost every day of their lives since they walked away from the Hudson alive. They wonder: Why am I still here? What am I meant to do with this second chance? As you read Bill's story, you will hear him refer to the crash as a wake-up call, and he is determined to answer it. He is in the midst of an awakening to life purpose, a process that can serve any of us at any time. If we tune into it.

—Kevin

In Bill's Words

LATE ON THE AFTERNOON OF JANUARY 15, I was riding in the back of the car of an undercover New York police officer. Sirens blaring and lights flashing, we raced through Midtown

Manhattan, like *Law and Order* without the handcuffs. The cop called his daughter and gushed, "You won't believe what I'm doing right now!"

How exciting is this? I thought. The Red Cross, countless firemen and police, the Port Authority, the FBI, the mayor, the governor, and their entourages had all swept in at the ferry terminal after we were plucked from the Hudson River. I was so pumped up that my blood pressure at the ferry terminal was 187 over 134! My boss, who had survived the crash with me, insisted that we bypass the airport hotel offered to us. "We will celebrate in style," he proclaimed, and as we checked in at the New York Helmsley, the concierge asked for my signature on an Internet photo of the rescue. When we headed to the nearest Gap to buy dry clothes and found the store closed, we tapped on the glass and were provided royal service. We enjoyed an elegant dinner complete with the best wine at the Capital Grille, where patrons approached us with hearty pats on the back, then topped it off with a Scotch with friends.

I excused myself to retreat to my room and call my wife, Amy, one more time. Then, alone for the first time, I suddenly felt exhausted. Within seconds I began to cry. The tears got bigger, the sobs heavier. *How close I came! How close Amy came to being a widow. How close my daughters, Katie and Lily, came to living the rest of their lives without a father. How close.* . . . In my mind I was back in the plane in that final minute as it descended toward the Hudson. "Brace for impact." I didn't stop crying for forty-five minutes.

The tears finally subsided long enough to fall into a deep but brief sleep. I really didn't want to get on a plane to go home the next day, so the plan was to take a train from New York to Washington early in the morning, rent a car, and drive back home to North Carolina. But CBS's *The Early Show* invited me on the next morning, and I knew that Amy wanted me home ASAP. "Amy, keep the girls home from school this morning so they can watch me on TV and see that I'm safe," I announced. "Then I'm flying home on the earliest available flight." I wanted my daughters to know in a very real way that I was still here. Nothing had ever seemed so important.

It was thirteen-year-old Katie who had answered the phone when I called from the life raft after trying to keep my balance on the slippery wing. "Katie, I'm in the Hudson River!" I shouted.

"What? Daddy, what's wrong?" she shouted back.

"No, it's all right. I've been in a plane crash but I'm in the Hudson now. I'm okay. Katie, I need to talk to Mom."

Amy told me later that within minutes, neighbors converged at our home to pitch in: helping seven-year-old Lily with her homework, cooking supper, cleaning up.

"I remember going around the house at dusk and closing all the blinds like I usually do," Amy adds. "Then I opened them again. I must have opened and closed them twenty times. I was in a daze."

The welcome-home parties were sweet. But those other feelings tracked me, too. The floodgates would open when I watched Katie receive an award from school, or Lily riding a horse, or when I drove by some familiar spot and thought how I might never have seen it again. I can be an emotional guy, and now almost anything could launch a river of tears.

I sought out a therapist to help sort out all these intense feelings. What did I gain from seeking professional help? That it was important to tell others how I felt, sharing not only the joy of having them in my life and gratitude for their love and support, but also my sadness and grief. All my feelings were natural and had a place. Now when I talk to my parents and grandparents, instead of telling them what I'm *doing*, I tell them how I'm *feeling*. With friends and family I try not to rely on e-mail and texting, where we can keep communication at arm's length. Now I get on the phone and talk. Do you ever wonder if maybe as a society we hunger for personal connection but don't know how to do it?

I realized that before the crash, I had probably been somewhat depressed, at times feeling lonely and sad, highly stressed. I suffer from alopecia areata, an inflammatory hair loss disease, and while doctors don't know exactly what causes it, stress might well be involved. But after becoming more accepting of my feelings and remembering that my family comes first, I was able to approach work with a clearer head. The hair is slowly coming back!

Still, there was something else I needed help sorting out. The bigger questions. "I feel this tremendous burden," I explained to my pastor. "I believe that I was spared for some reason, but I can't figure out what that reason, is. I can't help thinking I should be doing something, something big. But what?"

"Be a good parent to your kids," he replied. "Don't ever lose sight of how big that is. Also, you help run a company that employs four hundred people. That's a big contribution." I nodded but still appeared unconvinced. "You don't need to quit your job and run off to the seminary," he added. "If a door opens, you will know when to walk through it. But you don't need to drop everything to find out what that door is."

Comforted by those words, I turned my focus to being the best dad I could be. I'm far from perfect, but I have always tried to steer clear of being the kind of absentee parent I had known. My father divorced my mother when I was four, and for various painful reasons, I haven't seen him in twenty years. My stepfather was a wonderful father who worked hard to support us, and so he was not really involved in the day-to-day activities in the lives of my two brothers and me while we were growing up in Edgewood, Kentucky. He was a father of his generation; I want to be a father of my generation. That means offering the gift of time and, with my daughters, doing whatever they want to do. With Katie it might be camping and mountain biking, and with Lily it might mean pizza or ice cream after piano lessons.

I try hard never to miss a celebration or major event at school, and while more than likely I would have gone to those events before the crash, I would have felt anxiety about skipping out from work. As Chief Financial Officer for our international firm, I have many responsibilities. Now I choose to be with my girls because it just feels right. And when Lily feels a bit clingy and wants to lie on top of me on the sofa while watching TV, I open my arms wide.

With Amy, we've been on a high since January 15, where in the past we might have gotten caught up in petty things. Her support has been a salvation. She keeps a homemade chalkboard she bought at a church bazaar in our kitchen, and each week she puts up an inspirational saying there. One recent message: "Do not try to be better than everyone else; try to be the best person you can be."

I've continued to watch for those new doors, some way to give back the gift I have received, to answer the call, and I have found at least one. When I was asked if I would speak about my Flight 1549 experience to my church, St. Mark's Lutheran in Mooresville, I agreed. I soon received invitations from several other churches, and I've done my best to accommodate them. Here's a condensed version of my talk:

Have you ever asked yourself, Why am I here? Am I doing the right things with my life? Am I a good spouse, parent, child, or friend? Am I using the gifts God has given me for the best possible uses? Am I living my life as God wants me to live it? Do I need change in my life for more fulfillment and happiness?

Over the years, I have participated in studies and seminars directed toward finding our purpose, and I've used the knowledge gained, oh, for a while. More often than not, the handout material ends up on the bookshelf collecting dust, and over time most things revert back to the way they were. Well, my wake-up call came on January 15. It has been called the "Miracle on the Hudson," and to me it was a miracle and a message.

When I heard that pilot say, "Brace for impact," I thought I was going to die. Oddly enough, I do not recall being afraid of the physical part of dying because I was in God's hands. I was more afraid of what would happen to Amy, Katie, and Lily, afraid that I had not been the best husband, father, and friend that I could have been, that I had not somehow lived the full life that I always thought I would. And although I was on the plane with 155 people, I thought I was going to die alone—without being around my family and saying good-bye. So I had about forty-five seconds to pray, to ask for help and forgiveness and the continued blessing and welfare for my family. I was not thinking about my job, my material possessions, or anything like that.

As it turns out, none of us were alone. God was with all of us and in control of that plane. We were all blessed by God to survive that crash, and he has a plan/purpose for each of us. We all have work left to do, including those like you who were not on the plane but perhaps have been touched by this miracle. But what does God want me to do? Does receiving this gift of life mean quitting my job and going to seminary, leaving everything behind and becoming a missionary? Something radical?

Not necessarily. I believe it means I should reevaluate my actions and priorities, and maybe my personal goals, and place God at the top of the list. I think then that everything else will fall into place as he wants it to. Remember that Martin Luther said that there is no distinction between *sacred and secular work and that all honest vocations are sacred as long as one goes about their duties faithfully. Jesus was a carpenter and Mary cleaned houses.*

Also, I can share my love freely, without condition, with my family and my community. I can be a better listener, thinking of others first, being more proactive than reactive, more caring and thoughtful rather than critical and selfish. I can put the computer away and interact with my children. I can sit down and have a cup of coffee, or go for a walk with Amy. We can just talk. The best expression of love is time, and it is a precious gift because you only have a set amount of it. You really have no idea how much.

January 15, 2009, is a day that I will remember for the rest of my life. This is the day when any doubts I had about my faith in God were answered, when I realized I was the luckiest man alive to have met and married Amy, to have two fantastic daughters, and a wonderful extended family in this church. I have heard people say, "What would you do and how would you feel if you had one month to live? Would you have any regrets, would you have done God's work, would you be prepared? Do the people you love know you love them, not through your words but through your actions?"

Those are good questions to consider, but let me rephrase them a bit. What if you found out right now that you only had one minute left to live?

After one of my talks I was contacted by a husband and wife who heard me. "We have been estranged from our son and his family for nearly a year," they explained. "After listening to you, we reached out and broke the silence. Thank you for opening that door for us."

And then it dawned on me: while we are waiting to see what doors may open to us, or what our true purpose may be, we can be useful helping to open doors for others.

5
Lucille Palmer and Diane Higgins: ANGELS IN THE KITCHEN

The family is one of nature's masterpieces.

—George Santayana

Lenny, Lucille's husband, used to take the kids out into the backyard and point up at the planes. He'd say, "You'll never see me on one of those. Those wings don't have feathers!" True to his word, he never rode in an airplane. Lucille and her husband drove thousands of miles to kids' graduations, weddings, for visits, or just to travel. When Lenny died, twenty-seven years ago, Lucille was ready for flying, and so she did. She's been around the world. Lucille's is a big family and a close family. Lucille was eighty-five when the plane went down. She was with her daughter Diane, going to visit Diane's daughter Christine and Christine's two kids. Lucille has six children and many grandchildren and great-grandchildren. Diane is her middle daughter.

As I sit with Diane and Lucille in their home, at the kitchen table, a house surrounded by American flags, a tent in the back for a big barbecue, and angels all throughout the kitchen, I feel welcomed and at home. These are good people. Coffee is on, and Lucille and Diane and I sit to talk.

Soon Diane's sister comes in and she adds to the story, then so does Diane's husband, recently elected mayor of their New York town. "On my coattails," says Diane! After the accident, she became the town hero.

Jack, Diane's youngest, comes in next. He's twenty-one and tells me with tears in his eyes that January 15 was the worst day of his life and the best day of his life. He's making himself a hot dog while he talks. "I was upstate and it was like two directions for me," he explains. "I was upset because they were in a plane crash. I almost lost them. But on the same hand, how could I be upset? They were alive. It was a miracle." At his mom's request he shows me a picture he did of the plane in the river. He's an artist, to be sure. And he is a loving son. "But I had to go see them right away. It was the happiest moment in my life," he says. Jack is crying; so are all the rest of us. Diane says that Jack is her baby and they are deeply connected. And later, "Brian, my other son, is a mush, too! What can I say? I raised mushes!" The mayor walks through again, and I notice his T-shirt. "My Sons" it says, with a picture of two little boys.

And before I leave, Diane's daughter Christine calls on the phone, and Mom hands the phone to me. We talk as if we've known each other for years. She's the poet of the family. And these kind people that I have met are only a small part of this family! This family is in love, with one another, with their lives, with the gladness that they feel from not having lost Diane and Lucille . . . and happy, almost all the time, because of an earlier near tragedy

*involving Diane's daughter Susan that turned out equally
miraculous. They are in love. They are happy. They laugh,
and they cry. They tell stories and they tell jokes. "How'd
you like your vacation, Diane?"*

"It was eventful."

"What did you like better, the plane ride or the cruise?"

*"I'd have to say the cruise; the plane ride was kind of
short!"*

*And then there are the angels. When I left, they sent one
along with me, for my sister in the hospital. I took her
gladly and left her to help my sister.*

—Dorothy

In Lucille's Words

I'M NOT READY TO FLY AGAIN YET. I was on my way to my great-
grandson's first birthday, but now I'm thinking about a cruise.
I love the water. I just don't want to be in it!

I didn't really hear what the captain said over the intercom,
so I asked Diane. She said, "I love you, Mom. We're going down."

Wow. I was as calm as can be, in euphoria. I really wasn't
even there! When we hit, I said to Diane, "Go without me.
Go!" I've lived a good long life. I was ready to go.

But she wouldn't. She said, "No way, Ma. I'm not leaving
without you."

The window actually broke from the frame and landed in
my lap! I just pushed it over. When Diane convinced me she

wasn't leaving without me, I tried to get my purse. I figured when you're going somewhere you should have your purse. "No, Ma!" So I left it.

The stewardess, Donna, just took me under her wing to the front of the plane. I can still see her face. Even though there was a lot going on and clearly we were in trouble, I was calm. People helped me onto the raft and onto the ferry. Some man on the ferry took his own coat, a big warm one, and wrapped me and Diane in it and put his hat and scarf on me. He asked me if I wanted to call my husband. God bless him, whoever he was. He was a passenger on the ferryboat. Someone I'll never see again. Thank you to him, if he ever sees this.

Tears are beginning. Lucille is crying a bit; so is Diane.

We're the sob sisters in this family.

From the corner of the kitchen, Jack calls out, "I'll say!"

If I see a sad story on TV, I cry and let it all out. I think that's good for you. And I feel other people's pain and care about them, whether they're family or strangers. And so many people cared for me during the accident. And still there's a lot of laughter in our family. My son, who's a DJ, had us at an event, and he introduced me as Lulu who survived the Titanic and the Hindenburg and now the Miracle on the Hudson. He was playing the Beatles' song, "Lucy in the Sky with Diamonds." "Can't keep an old girl down!" he told them all. Pretty funny. We've all had a lot of laughs about this and a lot of cries, too. My philosophy about this is: It happened and I'm here! No trauma, no terrible reaction to it, but still we're the sob sisters. All of us cry at the drop of a hat. I'm not a worrier. How does worrying help anything? But I am religious, and I thank God every day, for everything. Lulu the great!

In Diane's Words

We were in seats 17 E and F. We were the last ones to board the plane, and there was Mom, being helped by the flight attendant Donna, walking down the aisle like a queen when we boarded. We were going to visit my daughter Christine. I was so worried about you, Mom!

"I was never worried," Lucille responds.

I worried enough for the two of us. I could see the buildings as we went down. That's a scary thing. *I hope it's quick.* That's what I thought. The water was coming up to our knees, but I don't think Mom noticed. She has trouble with the feeling in her legs, so I guess it was a good thing right then. "Please help me with my mother!" I yelled after we landed. That's where Donna came in. She had taken Ma onto the plane, and now she was helping her get off the plane. One of the angels. Everyone was wonderful, and everyone helped us and helped one another. I called my husband from the ferry, huddled up in that warm coat from that wonderful gentleman—a commuter on the ferry, I guess. My husband got the call, and then he called our daughter and said, "The plane has crashed!" My poor Christine! Her heart just stopped, until Dad said, "Everyone is okay." He should have done it the other way around. He called everyone: my brothers and sister, my other daughter and our sons.

A few days later, we saw Captain Sullenberger on TV and we just sat there holding one another and crying. I didn't think I'd get so emotional about it. But I do. Even now, as you can see. I was really surprised to hear that the captain spent sleepless nights after the flight, second-guessing himself. How could he have done any better? Mom wants to invite him to dinner!

We actually got home pretty quickly, since we're right in New York, but Mom got very sick and ended up in the hospital. We didn't know if it was from the accident or not, but she got back to being her old self pretty quickly, and within a few days she was out and about, eating at restaurants, shopping. Funny thing, though, and I guess this is the kind of family we are, after this big tragedy or near tragedy and within minutes of the event, we're finding things to laugh about. On shore when they were doing triage, checking us out to see how we were, they put tags around everybody's neck. That's how other medical people know we've been seen to, and they can check the tag to see if we need anything. I, of course, noticed that the tags included one category: *deceased*. "I'm glad they didn't check that one, Mom!" We laughed at that and a lot of other things . . . and we still do. And suddenly I saw my husband's doctor, Ray Basri! What a small world. He's an emergency rescue doctor. He came over and took pictures and checked us out. And a few days later he came to our house with champagne! How sweet is that?

When the investigators came, clearly worrying about whether this was a terrorist thing, I whispered to Mom, "The suits are here!" We know how to take things seriously and have a little fun with them at the same time. My husband told us (he has a slightly strange sense of humor, too), "Your plane went so close to the George Washington Bridge, the EZ Pass went off!"

When we got home, the media was calling. I agreed to a video for the local channel, and then I realized I had no makeup. It was at the bottom of the Hudson. I quickly called my daughter next door. "Help, bring makeup!" I didn't know if I wanted to keep talking about this. I was mixed about that. But people wanted to know.

I work as a nurse for our county health department, and the day after the accident, I got our newsletter about a presentation on "Psychological Effects on Survivors and Rescuers of a Trauma." Wow, how's that for coincidence? They invited me to speak. I'm not a public speaker, but I decided to tell my story. It was cathartic to talk about it. It was good for me, and I hope helped other people.

"She was marvelous," Lucille adds. "I heard her. She was so articulate and wonderful! She was so great."

Well, I'm just talking from the heart. Just telling my story.

It's amazing the people who come into our lives. Out of the blue, a World War II veteran that I used to take care of when I was a visiting nurse called me and asked if I would speak to a friend of his. I said I would, and an older man, a Jewish soldier from World War II, came to tell me about how he had ditched his plane and been captured. It was a terrible experience, of course. But he said he'd never talked about it when he came home. And that was not good for him. Finally, years later, one of his grandkids had to interview someone from the war, and so they talked to him. It was the first time he ever talked about this frightening experience. Then he began to talk about it more, and now he has a presentation he gives. He came to teach me what he had learned: that it is important to talk about it, important to share with others, for their sakes and for our own.

I've been through worse emotional stuff, though, and that's where the angels come in. My brother Drew said after the landing, "Believe in angels. Because there had to be angels." And there must be. When my daughter Susan was in a nearly-fatal car accident ten years ago, I was at the hospital praying. I asked for a sign that she would be okay . . . and when I looked up there on the wall was a mural with clouds and an angel. A feeling of peace came over me then. But later, complications set in and she was at risk again.

Debbie comes in: "I'd gotten this book at the mall, on a whim: Anglespeake. I'd given it to Diane's daughter when she was in the hospital. I had a deep experience of hearing

angels speak to me . . . in the mall of all places. I was buy-
ing the book again, since I'd given her my first copy, and I
was sitting down to look at it in the food court when I heard
two people talking next to me. I heard one of them say,
"Everything's going to be okay." I turned to see who they
were and no one was there. I knew Susan would be okay."

I was in recovery with Susan, and the lights were dim. She woke a bit and said, "Why don't you read this book Aunt Debbie gave me?" And as I read the book, it said everything I needed to hear. I just opened up to see what would happen, and there I was talking to an angel . . . and her name was Dixie! I don't know why. They tell you in the book to ask their names, so I did. And I don't really understand all this, but it surely felt true. That night I woke up in the middle of the night with the thought: *complete recovery by May 3.* And she was. So we've been an angel family ever since then. You can see how many I have in the kitchen alone! And when the *New York Daily News* had a cartoon by Bill Bramhall of the plane being held up by angels, I couldn't believe it. But these weren't cherub angels. They were Hells Angels angels. Mom told a reporter who interviewed her how much she loved the cartoon, so he sent us the original. There it is!

It got really emotional for us only after the accident, in the hospital when everyone came to visit. The physical contact and being with all the family just made us all cry and break down. It was healing. And so has the sharing been, with family and other people . . . and just being together.

But really, it was my daughter Chris who brought it all home. She always writes poems for every family event. And they always make everyone laugh and cry. It's amazing. Here's the poem she wrote. I can't read it out loud.

Lucille and sister Debbie, in unison: "Neither can I!"

On an unexpected note, I (Dorothy) read the poem out loud. Or tried to. As I read, we all cried. And sometimes we laughed. And Lucille could be seen laughing and crying at the same time. The poem is about family and miracles and angels. It is a poem that tells a very deep story about this family . . . with a touch of their ever-present humor!

But I have learned a few things in this experience. The first is to stop. My experience with angels when Susan was so injured, that was my awakening. But it's so easy to get caught up in life and lose track of what's really important, and now I can stop myself and say, "This is *not* important." I don't always do it, but I do it more now. I'm living closer to the things I really care about. Family is the most important. And being kind to others and welcoming them into your life, however they show up. Everybody has bad things happen to them. What was Dad's expression? Mom?

Lucille: "Life is what you make it!"

Yep, and that's what we're all trying to do. Make it good.

Angels Riding Shotgun

Christine Griggs

[Christine is Diane's daughter, Lucille's granddaughter, the one they were
going to visit when the plane went down.]

Dedicated with love to Mom and Lulu.

Everybody knew
that Lenny never flew.
Not in any kind of weather,
didn't trust "those wings without feathers."
And he never did, 'til one day in July,
when he was called to His home beyond the sky.
And now everybody knew,
that Lenny finally flew.
There are angels flying shotgun
There are angels next to me
There are angels flying shotgun
I'm as safe as I could be.
The call came late.
and like a twist of fate,
her life wouldn't be the same
but she'd get her daughter through the pain.
She'd meet the ambulance that was on its way
to the hospital, and she began to pray:
Let there be angels riding shotgun
Let there be angels close to her
Let there be angels riding shotgun
Please grant this prayer from a mother.

They boarded Flight 1549,
not knowing in a matter of time,
that they'd all be changed,
their priorities rearranged,
by a flock of birds
and three little words.
"Brace for impact" they heard the pilot say,
unaware of all their "helpers" that day:
There were angels flying shotgun
There were angels all around
There were angels flying shotgun
They helped Sully ease them down.
Landing on the river
frigid water made them shiver
but from every side,
more rescuers had arrived.
To pull them out, to lead the way,
to let them know, they would be okay.
And now everybody knew
about Sully and his crew,
and what they did that day
and the changes prayer can make.
There are angels riding shotgun
They were there for all to see
There were angels riding shotgun
And some look like you and me.

6
Warren Holland:
REMEMBERING WHAT MATTERS

For by grace are ye saved through faith; and that
not of yourselves: it is the gift of God: Not of works,
lest any man should boast.

—Ephesians 2:8–9
(the last words spoken by Warren's great-grandfather)

Three months to the day after Warren Holland crash-
landed in the Hudson, his eleven-year-old son, Warren, was
hit by a car while he was crossing the street to school.
Warren Junior bounced to the hood of the car and sustained
only a few bumps and bruises. And shortly after that,
Warren Senior had an emergency appendectomy. Days after
that surgery, as we talked, Warren remembered his great-
grandfather's last words scribbled on the inside cover of an
old Bible, which he came across while looking for answers
in the aftermath of his ordeal. These verses had now become
so powerful to Warren himself and to Warren's son. Warren
tells me that the answer to the big question "Why me, why
was I saved?" is, for Warren, even more poignantly "Why
was my son saved?" The answer comes in the next line of
this same Bible verse his great-grandfather quoted on his

death bed: "For we are his workmanship, created in Christ Jesus unto good works, which God hath before ordained that we should walk in them" (Eph. 2:10).

Facing death, and living beyond his near-death experience, has brought Warren to the big questions and to the importance of how he lives his life every day. And he has his answers. He also knows how easy it is to forget what he has learned, and his deepest hope and intention is not to forget, not to get lost, as it is so easy to do, in the hubbub of life, the stress, the anxiety, the lists, and the "white noise." Speaking at his church, he tells the crash story, of course, but what he says, amidst laughter of recognition by the many people attending, tells the deeper story.

"Before this, I'd be sitting in church on Sunday, listening to the speaker, telling myself that I'll be a really great dad from now on. That would last until about 6 AM Monday morning!"

Warren understands that this is the real work, remembering.

—Dorothy

In Warren's Words

I WAS ON AN EARLIER FLIGHT than I'd ever been on. I was scheduled for 7:00 in the evening, but it was snowing. When I was meeting with my boss, he said, "Warren, what are you still doing here? It's snowing. Go home!" So I wound up on Flight 1549. By the time we had heard the thud, I thought,

Bomb. . . . This can't be happening to me. This is not in the plan. I went back and forth with waves of calm and prayer and then despair again. When I realized the plane had no power, I just prayed intensely. *Please, God, help us, please, God, forgive me.* Then I'd think, *Maybe we'll get an engine started.* Then, as we kept getting lower and lower, it was real fear, and I realized I was likely going to die on that airplane. I turned to God. I can't remember what I said, but I felt as close to God as I've ever been.

When I spoke to my church sometime after the accident, I didn't prepare anything—hadn't thought much about it—but I said some things that I realize were important about my closeness to God at that moment of near death: "I didn't bargain with him. I didn't say if you get me out of this I will . . . fill in the blank. I prayed for my family, for my children, and for my wife. And in the midst of that utter hopelessness, I was looking forward, as crazy as that may sound, to finding out about death. What's death going to be like? Complete darkness, bright light, perfect clarity, joy, salvation? What's it going to be like in the presence of God? I'm nothing special, but God gives us all hope in the direst of moments, that sense of hope and salvation. . . . Right at the end I tried to turn my BlackBerry on to give my kids something for closure. It was password protected, and I couldn't get the damn thing on! As the water got closer, I put it down. . . . I hated to leave them like that."

We hit with a thud, and at that moment I got the most serious injury I was to sustain in this whole accident. My

BlackBerry flew up, hit me on the bridge of my nose, and nearly knocked me out! I never saw it again. And I don't mind.

Once I got out, it was a clear blue day, beautiful, and the water taxi was on its way. Having gone back and forth during the crash between optimism and despair, I realized that this was a huge take-away lesson that I needed to really *get*.

After the accident, I had a sense of peace and quiet that was amazing. I had immediately anticipated the euphoria and the good will that would follow. That seemed like the clear outcome. But I knew early on that it would dissipate. I can feel the noise encroaching again, and that's what I'm fighting. My goal is to make space for that peace and quiet that I know is waiting for me.

People always ask me about contacting family. *When did you get in touch with your wife?* It was a funny story, really, though no one laughed then. I called my wife from a ferryboat passenger's cell phone. I said, "Honey, the plane went down in the Hudson. Everyone's okay, though." She was carpooling. I could hear the kids making noise. She told me she was glad everyone was all right. But she sounded confused, as in *Why is he telling me this?* I said, "Gotta go, it's not my phone." And I could hear her gasp. She got it. I hadn't told her I was on an early flight, but then she knew.

As a family, we've been really committed to counting our blessings and not getting caught in the unimportant things in life since then. And of course, to remind us, our son was hit, and it was another near-death experience. My son was scared by that, as I was by my experience. He doesn't like to walk to school anymore. I can understand that. But it's brought us closer. We're both survivors. I shared the Ephesians verse with him, and he decided to read the Bible all the way through. It's a little harder than he thought, but he does think about these important things more. He has a bit more insight than your typical eleven-year-old. He's also more introspective. And I think he understands my experience in a way that other kids wouldn't. He's been there. So all of us focus on our lives in the present, not dwelling on what could have been. I carry a sense of peace and gratitude that pervades everything.

Of course, as I talked about in my speech, I have to work at it. I still get anxious and uptight and short-tempered. But now I have . . . a circuit breaker! Within a minute or two I remember what's important, what I really value, and I don't stay wound up. Used to be that one difficulty would build on another—each annoyance creating a smoldering ball of nerves. People would have said, and I'd have agreed, that I was high-strung and intense. I don't think they'd say that now. I'm a more pleasant person to be around. Now when I'm annoyed by three children, I think almost immediately, *How wonderful to be annoyed by three precious children!*

I do work in a high-stress environment, especially these days, at a bank in the financial markets, in the worst economic environment since the Great Depression. And that weighed heavily on me. But this episode makes those last six months bearable. This has taken the tension out of my work. All of it is self-created stress—understandable, but still self-created. Interestingly, I work more efficiently now and with less aggravation. *Lessen your stress, and all is easier.* It's that simple . . . though of course, as I know only too well, it's not as simple as it sounds.

But I work at remembering and doing good works. I never had the feeling I needed to change my whole life and go save the world. But this experience is my message, my ministry, my mission. People ask me about it all the time, and I stop to tell them, not just the "brace for impact" story, but the deeper story, the real impact. The lessons of how to live a good life; what to be thankful for. I talked about this a bit in my church speech. Not to share that would be an opportunity wasted, one that might potentially impact someone else's life in a positive way.

I've mostly kept out of the limelight, though. I don't like public speaking. My ministry is in these small acts, at home, with friends, with strangers . . . with enemies. It's easy to be a good friend to a friend. It's not easy to be a good friend to people you don't like or are a threat to you or just annoy you. That's the real work. That's where I try now to be a good friend. I don't have to be front and center. The acquaintance with an illness or the individual who's lonely, these are the people who are important, whom I try to reach out to now. Instead of a passing feeling of sympathy, I ask myself if I can help. Can I be part of the solution, for whatever this issue is, for whatever person it's affecting?

I do have a calling now. I'm glad to have this chance to share it. It's about contentment with what you have . . . about living life so there are no regrets. It's the promise of a sense of peace that comes not from making a good living or the like, but from being in peace. It's been important for me to make this experience meaningful. I don't want to preach, but I am continuing to look for answers. Some of them come in my day-to-day life. I've always tried to live a balanced life, but it's hard. Now I am more aware, more careful. I pay more attention. Doing yard work in the hot Charlotte summer is now a pleasure, not a chore. Having a deep conversation is a joy, not a distraction from things on my list. I do enjoy my job, and now I enjoy it more because I have more of a sense of larger meaning. I'm taking stock of my life. I hope others do as well. I had a very profound couple of minutes on that plane. But it's the many months of soul- searching that have followed that are really important. I've been blessed to have this experience. This will guide my life.

7
Darren Beck:
CIRCLE OF LOVE

Love life and life will love you back.
Love people and they will love you back.

—Arthur Rubinstein

Parents know the guilty feeling. Somehow, some way, we were not fully there for our children. We didn't step up when we were really needed, and the pain our children suffers, whether real or only what we imagine, tears at our own hearts. Doesn't matter how or why we couldn't come through. We just failed. And the sting only goes away, if it does at all, when we find a way to really come through the next time, and the time after that.

For the parents onboard Flight 1549, a different version of this feeling has been playing out since their joyous return to their families. They think: *we almost lost our chance to ever be there for our kids!* So, like Darren Beck, they vow to fully utilize this second chance to love 'em like they've never loved 'em before. Darren has three sons, and he knows he was a good dad before the crash, but he is determined to become an even better dad now. He's finding lots of ways to

*do that. I can appreciate just what that opportunity means
to him when he brings up Father's Day during our talk.
You'll see that in his story.*

*But there's another side to the whole realm of being there
for our children that Darren also has needed to learn and experience. It's the part of the equation that any of us may do well
to remember, especially for those times that, due to our other
life commitments or our health, we can't always show up for
our kids the way we want to. As Darren comes to understand,
it doesn't mean that we've failed. It doesn't mean that the circle
of love has been broken. If we pay attention, we even may see
the opportunity for the circle to grow ever wider because a part
of giving is the ability to also receive.*

—Kevin

In Darren's Words

AS JUNE 10 APPROACHED, I faced one of those dilemmas every
working parent dreads. My oldest son, Tyler, would be graduating from Ballantyne Elementary School in Charlotte that
day, and I had to be there. On the same day, my employer was
filming a new TV commercial in Los Angeles as a crucial part of
our company's major rebranding campaign. As Chief Marketing
Officer, I had to be there.

What was I to do? When I survived the plane crash of Flight
1549, I made a vow to always be there for my family. Oh, I had
never been one of those a-hundred-hours-per-week work guys

who never sees his family, but I certainly had those moments when I would choose a work meeting over some family event. Don't most of us make those choices sometimes? When Tyler's school held those little celebrations at the end of second grade, third grade, and fourth grade, I didn't always make it. But after escaping from the brink of death, my time with my family seemed too precious to relegate to second choice. I was going to make sure I was there for anything important, and to make more important anything we did together. Like that recent Saturday when I had errands to run at Home Depot. In the past I'd simply take Tyler and his younger brothers, Gage and Colin, along with me and take care of business. Time, but not quality time. Instead, I postponed my errand and took them to the sporting goods store where I bought all four of us new baseball mitts.

Tyler's graduation was bigger than a baseball mitt. I had it marked on my calendar for weeks. It's true that I had never cared much for graduation myself, even skipping my own college ceremony. But this was my *son*. And yet, my whole twenty-five-member marketing team and entire organization was counting on me to help guide a successful shoot, and aligning the quirky schedules of director, cast, and studio time was even more complicated than arranging drop-offs and pick-ups in a household with three boys. *Family or work? Work or family?* Did my vow really mean something or didn't it?

"Darren, you need to be there for your son's graduation," my CEO said. "We'll change the date somehow, or I'll go there in your place."

It was a generous offer from a supportive boss, but the real answer didn't firmly take hold until I sat down with Tyler to discuss various options.

"Dad, I don't need to go to that graduation," he told me. "I want you to take me with you to LA."

"Take you with me? Tyler, are you sure?" I asked.

"Yeah, Dad, you know I like acting. It will be fun."

So I agreed. I don't know if I could have put my finger on the "why." Maybe I was learning that part of being there for your family after a near-death experience is to recognize that your family also really wants to be there for *you*. Tyler was my teacher. This was the same son who surprised me with a gift when I woke him up the morning after I had flown back from New Jersey the night of the crash. After watching the news of our miracle landing, Tyler had carefully wrapped up the red, white, and blue ribbon he had earned at a junior triathlon competition.

"Dad, you need a good luck charm when you fly in an airplane again," he explained. That medal has been tucked safely inside my travel bag for every flight since then.

Now Tyler had given me something new, a plan to hold up both family and work commitments and do so in a way that would give us an opportunity to become even closer. Now I just had to figure out how to make the plan work. Tyler and his brothers had flown with their mom and me to Los Angeles when I was invited on *The Ellen DeGeneres Show* with seven other Flight 1549 passengers. I had insisted that my entire family got to fly with me, or I would not go on the show. It worked out, and I needed them. I have to admit I was feeling pretty shaky my first time back in the air. My family was there to support me, and I could be there to hug my six-year-old Gage when he asked, "Daddy, what if the geese come back?" But flying as a family on an adventure was much different from flying solo with your eleven-year-old son on an important business trip.

Also, the filming meant twelve-plus-hour days of my focused attention in what can be a high-pressured environment. My plan was to park Tyler in the corner of the filming room with a stash of books. He loves reading so much, he devoured all seven books we gave him last Christmas by New Year's. But how would some director who probably rules over his dominion with an iron fist react to a kid invading his turf?

I was a little nervous when Tyler and I arrived for the preshoot meeting. The conference table looked like something set up for King Arthur and his knights, and when all the principal players gathered round, Tyler was stationed quietly in the corner.

"Tyler, come up here to this table right now," the director suddenly instructed, as he motioned for an assistant to bring in another chair. "You're going to sit with us."

Tyler didn't hesitate to take his place, and he didn't miss a beat when the director turned to him midway through the planning session and said in his most serious Hollywood tone, "Tyler, what do you think about all of this?"

"Well," Tyler began, "just remember: the client is always right."

The room reverberated with laughter. I laughed, too, but

my eyes were getting a bit watery. The next day's shoot lasted fourteen hours. This time, I had given Tyler a Zune video player to keep him occupied. He never touched it. He was entranced by it all: the cameras, the actors' preparations, the director's instructions, the same motions and the same lines executed over and over and over again. During breaks, that same kindhearted director made sure that Tyler got a chance to look through the camera lens and have his photo taken in his director's chair.

By the way, the commercial turned out great.

In our short downtime before heading home, we rode bikes to the beach and tested the roller coaster on the Santa Monica pier. Just a dad and his son enjoying an adventure together. Out there in warm and sunny southern California, 3,000 miles from the Hudson River, no one watching us could imagine how a whole lifetime of shared adventures had been so, so close to being snuffed out. I still can't imagine it sometimes either.

In my own childhood, family was often all I had. I was born in Salt Lake City but grew up in Colorado, Hawaii, California, and Florida before returning to Utah to graduate from high school. Everyone always assumed I was an Army brat, but my father actually worked for State Farm Insurance and had always been willing to relocate. With a move popping up every couple of years, making friends was futile. Painfully shy, I gravitated to my parents and three older brothers and older sister. Somehow, my family gave me just enough of what I needed. I stayed in Utah long enough to meet my wife, Tara, and earn both an undergraduate degree and an MBA from Brigham Young University. Then I left Utah and began my own adult travels: to Bentonville, Arkansas, for a stint with Walmart; to Oregon; to San Diego; and now to Charlotte—all before turning forty. Now it was my own family sustaining me.

After the crash, Tara and I leaned on each other during the emotional ups and downs we shared, though not necessarily at the same time. The Saturday after the crash, we managed to get someone to watch the three boys so we could go out to dinner alone. Tara was in tears the entire time as the reality of what might have been sunk in. "Is there anything I can do?" the waiter kept asking, probably figuring we were breaking up. Tara also has been there for me in my own vulnerable moments, and I have had many of them. I used to be the tough guy, but when you are told you are about to die and then you walk away unharmed, it changes your perceptions. So I am softer now, and that's totally fine.

I also have discovered a new kind of family. I launched the Yahoo! group of Flight 1549 passengers, which I admit was partly a selfish act. I loved the e-mail distribution list that Glenn Carlson had helped to grow, but with dozens of e-mails flying around every day, some passengers began to become overwhelmed and drop out of the list. In a Yahoo! group, I knew I could control the flow and keep everyone happy. I asked Glenn to co-moderate with me, and the group has become a fixture in all our lives.

Now I have this bizarre emotion for 150 people I didn't

even know a few months ago. In February when I was interviewed on *Larry King Live* with Beth McHugh and some other passengers, I said, "I'd consider giving Beth a kidney if she needed one because I love her that much now." When I say things like that, I'm joking but I'm not joking.

It's amazing to me that I not only survived the plane crash but that I shared the experience with Don and Ben, two members of my marketing team. We don't usually travel together because they're both on the technical side, but they were needed for meetings in New York with a company we were considering buying that January. I wound up checking them in for Flight 1549 on a borrowed laptop. They had initially been assigned seats well in the rear, but I tried to move them up as I always do for myself. I got Don onto a window seat on the exit row, and as most of our fellow passengers know, he was instrumental in getting that door open and free almost immediately after Sully landed that Airbus on the water. "I put you on that wing, Don," I kid him. "I saved your life." Truth is, his alert act helped save many.

Most visitors to our office know all about our adventure on the Hudson. I even had a large trophy made with a replica of our Airbus inside. When we received our belongings back from US Airways, I got my laptop, though it was corroded beyond repair. Instead of throwing it away, I put it up on a corner of my desk as a reminder. Recently a coworker accidentally spilled water all over it. "Oh, I'm so sorry," she said. I smiled and said, "Don't worry, you can't do anything to it that hasn't already been done."

That's the kind of moment we share with one another in our office, in the Yahoo! group, throughout this big new second family I belong to. It keeps us going, keeps us together. Still, it is my own family of five that feeds me. When I thought about Father's Day approaching recently and the time we would get to share, I had one of those all-choked-up moments again. I'll probably keep having them. I will keep to that vow to be there for them, and I will do my best to appreciate how they will be there for me—whatever it takes or however it comes out.

Soon after we returned from Tyler's Hollywood debut, my son gave me a glimpse of how that might look. "So, Dad," he asked, "what are we going to do for my high school graduation?"

8
Michele Davis:
FAMILY TIES

*Michele, who is just twenty-four, has a few tattoos. One
of them, around her wrist, says "a Bushel and a Peck." She
got this tattoo because she loves her mother and grandmother . . . and because she's young, likes tattoos, had pink
hair at the time of the crash, and generally is a sparkly,
happy young person. Why this tattoo? Her mother used to
sing her that song, and her grandmother used to sing it to
her mother, and by the time Michele was a teenager, instead
of the usual "'Bye, I love you" at the end of visits or phone
calls, the grandmother, mother, and daughter all had a
shorthand: "A bushel and a peck!" The song was written in
1950 and made popular with the Broadway play (then
movie) Guys and Dolls:*

I love you, a bushel and a peck!

A bushel and a peck and a hug around the neck!

*What brings a family so close together that a young per-
son tattoos "I love you, Mom" (in her particular version of*

that phrase) on her wrist? This family has that magic something, and a near tragedy like Flight 1549 makes it all the more evident. No one says the family is perfect or there were no troubles growing up—not at all. They have had their share of ups and downs, but along the way, through their shorthand words of love, through songs sung to children at night, through their ongoing connections, they kept alive what was most important.

Talking to Michele by phone, I know her grandmother is in the room with her. I've already spoken to Susan, Michele's mom, and Eva, her grandmother. Both Mom and Grandma shared their lively humor, their happiness, and their love of Michele with me. As Michele and I talk, I can hear laughter at something Michele has said, sounds of agreement, a sigh or two, and I think I hear a little crying from Grandma when Michele herself gets a little teary.

Michele wanted nothing more after that crash in New York than to get back to her mom and her own home in Washington state. And now, these few months later, Michele is moving to New York to try out a new life. What a powerful set of values: connection and autonomy, closeness and freedom, being able to say hello and good-bye. This is interdependence, the delicate balance of loving and letting go. These are the ties that bind.

—Dorothy

In Michele's Words

I'VE ALWAYS FREAKED OUT ON PLANES. I never liked them. I've been known to cancel my flight because I psyched myself out about it. When I fly, I'm the one who is clinging to the chair arms, jumping at every bump. When the airline offered to send me home right away, I didn't go. I thought I'd never get on a plane again. I was in New York visiting my boyfriend, Paul, and I got this flight at the last minute, and it was the last seat, and it was in the back, 24D, and I didn't like that at all. I kept looking around to see if there was an empty seat I could move into. But unusually, I wasn't very scared. I don't know why. Paul had dropped me off; I'd gotten a book to read. I figured I'd fall asleep on the plane. On the plane, I got my travel pillow and settled in. I know the flight safety instructions by heart, so I didn't even worry about that.

In the back we couldn't see what was going on. Even the flight attendant didn't know. We all heard the boom, and I thought maybe it was an exploding coffee pot or something. When it was clear we were going down, I reached out to the woman next to me. I was so scared. I was running thoughts in my head. *This can't be happening to me.* They say that your past flashes before you, but it was my future that was flashing before me: the future I thought I wouldn't have. *I want to see my niece grow up. . . . I want to have babies, see my mom, marry a good man. I want to see my grandma! . . . This can't be it!*

This must all have happened pretty fast. The young woman next to me, I don't know her name, an African

American woman, was praying out loud. When I grabbed her hand she said, "We're going to be fine. We have angels on this plane." The thoughts shifted a bit, I remember, probably as I got to the point of thinking I was going to die. *I don't know if my mom can handle this. I hope she does . . . and Grandma. I don't want to die and hurt these people that I love.* I thought about my younger sister and older brother.

I am my mother's favorite!

Here, the sound of laughter can be heard in the background. The one-liner, a break in her story, slows some of the emotion and brings Michele back to her sense of safety and to the closeness and humor that her family uses to show their love. But the story continues in just a moment.

The impact, a violent car crash. The back of the plane got it worst. I saw water rush up the side of the plane. *Oh. My God! Quick, check my body. Am I hurt?. . . I'm fine!*

All in all the rest was scary but quick. Visions of *Titanic* floated through my head, 'cause we were all stuck in the back, and I couldn't see that emergency exits had opened. I saw a man with his little girl, and I started shouting, "Hurry up, there's a kid back here!" It was gray, nasty water rising up. On the life raft, I'm sorry to say, I wasn't one of the strong, together folks helping everybody to get calm. In fact, a really nice guy helped calm me down. The wounded flight attendant got on our raft, and I had the presence of mind to give her my scarf to tie around her leg. We were throwing extra life vests to people still on the wings and putting ours on. I had only a seat cushion, which I remembered to grab from first class. But another nice guy helped me put on an actual life vest.

These were the most beautiful strangers ever! And I was happy to meet my seatmate at the emergency site and to give her a big hug. I wish I knew her name. You know my only injury? A scar on my thumb where we held hands so tightly that I must have gotten cut by a fingernail! Don't know whether it was hers or my own. But before that, on the raft, I had to call my mom. I called her before the flight, right before. I *always* do. Hers was the only number I had memorized—not even my boyfriend's! "*Mama, mama, mama! My plane's crashed into the river. I'm on the lifeboat. I'm okay.*"

The governor, or mayor, or maybe both came to where we were, but all I wanted was a familiar face. *I'd rather see my mom*, I thought. But just then Paul, my boyfriend, came in. I don't know how they found him. I hadn't called him, but there he was, on the other side of the taped-off area. I jumped across that line, bawling my eyes out.

I don't feel like I'm dealing with this all that well. They used to call me "JELL-O Girl" at the bar where I work. I served JELL-O shots. But not because of that so much as that I was always bubbly, jumpy—the crazy happy girl with pink hair and tattoos. People would say, "She must be on happy pills!" But I was just happy. All of this went away. I didn't go to work for two weeks. I just hung out with my mom. Oh, I finally did get back from New York to Washington, but only because the airline paid for Paul to travel with me

. . . and they gave me some antianxiety meds!

When I got back to work, there was a party, and everyone was great, and I started working again. But I wasn't the same. I was doing "strong," but I didn't feel strong . . . or happy. I had five hundred emotions going on in me. One night I finally broke down. I was talking to this guy, and it was his birthday, and on the TV behind me was more about the flight. A friend saw that I was shaken and just took me away to let me break down. She said something I'll never forget. *"Every-body has a plane crash. You just have to figure out how to deal with it."* That's what I've been doing ever since, and I know some really good things are coming out of it. But they haven't come quickly.

For a while I was so negative. And there were people who showed a lot of caring, and others who were really insensitive. Just strangers, kind of grabbing at me, wanting the story. I got so dark I broke up with Paul. But it was about flying and my mood, not us, and now we're together again. I'm reaching out to people when I have a bad day. And I've flown to see him, though once I drove. The flight attendants on that first flight were so wonderful!

I haven't always lived near my family. I've lived in lots of places since I was eighteen. I'd get an urge to try something and go for it. But I always came home. Now I've been living, for a while, with my mom, after my apartment lease ended. My family loves me. It's nice to know you can come back home if you need to.

I know some things that have changed in me forever. Don't

sweat the small stuff is one of the major learnings. I took life for granted before . . . and people. Now I make sure everybody knows I love them, and I tell them. I don't think I've missed one opportunity to tell someone that I cared, and that is very different and feels great.

One of the coolest things, and I have a video, is that Mom went out after all of this and got the same tattoo on her wrist as mine. I'd been asking her forever. "Mom, you should get the same one!" She didn't have any tattoos. It's not really her thing, and she really didn't like the idea of the pain. But after I got home (from the crash), I said jokingly, "When you going to get your tattoo, Mom?" and she said she was going to.

"What's a little pain compared to you being safe?" she said.

I bought the tattoo for her for her birthday and Mother's Day, and now we have matching tattoos of *a Bushel and a Peck!*

Grandma yells in the background, "Not me!"

My grandpa was a sailor. His ninetieth birthday was on the day of the crash. I think about my whole, large family, and I love them all. I've reconnected with some of my siblings on my dad's side since the accident. My half sister Marie heard about the accident, and though we hadn't been in touch for years, she called my grandma to find out if I was okay. That was the only way my dad found out about it—through her. I just went to her wedding and got to connect with lots of other family members. I don't know if that would have happened without this.

But I'm especially close to my mom and grandma. They're pains in the butt . . .

Grandma is laughing in the background.

. . . but I love them to death!

Thankfully, for this family, not to death.

Generations

"The Eggs are in the Basket!" Michele Davis's mom, Susan, shoots me a quick e-mail to let me know her daughter Michele is safe and sound in New York. The eggs are in the basket? Yep, that's another one of the shorthand phrases that Michele and her family use to tell one another they have arrived safely. Susan has her own trauma story of that day. It begins with her daughter calling from an unknown number. Late and at work, Susan looks at the number and thinks "telemarketer," but her heart answers the phone. "Mama, mama, mama!" And Susan begins to sob. Colleagues at work get on the Internet and TV to learn more news. Susan calls her mother.

"Mama, Michele's plane crashed in the river. . . . She's okay," Susan stammers.

"You could have told me that first," Eva replies, but hearing her sobbing daughter, she responds in a firm and loving motherly way. "Susan Marie . . . Susan Marie. Michele is okay."

Susan heads home thinking about her daughter, with no phone, in the middle of the Hudson somewhere . . . or maybe on the shore. There is no way to know for sure. Susan almost takes the airport exit to jump on a plane to New York . . . .

Susan is no longer taking life for granted. "I call my dad a lot now. He's ninety, and I just call to tell him I love him," she relates. "And I have my tattoo. It did hurt, but now Michele is always with me."

I ask Susan how old she and her mom are. "I'm forty-four, but Mom is always twenty-nine. She's actually—" But I promise not to say.

I also get a phone call from Eva, Michele's grandmother. A singing phone call! "I just called to say I love you. I just called to say I care!" This is a Stevie Wonder song, and this is their greeting. Sung in grandma voices, daughter voices, and granddaughter voices. By the end of the phone call, Eva has me singing it, too! Eva spends some time with her daughter Susan on the phone now, almost every day. Susan has a two-hour commute, and so they use that time to catch up. Susan has an earphone to make it safe . . . as do all the family members. Eva gave them to everyone. "I make Michael wear his!" Michael is Eva's grandson, Michele's brother. He drove his sister Michele all the way to New York from Washington. And he's about to have a baby. And he wears his earphone 'cause Grandma wants him to. This is a family that stays in touch, stays in love: "A family epidemic of love."

Eva tells me that Michele has a new lease on life. Her old bubbly self has returned. "When you told her it was *okay to cry, it changed everything for her," she tells me. I can't say how very happy that makes me.*

—Dorothy

9
Mark Hood:
SOLDIER OF FAITH

Always lead from the front, and leadership is a two-way street, with respect running both ways.

—Captain Sully Sullenberger, offering advice to Mark Hood
for a lecture about leadership to cadets at The Citadel

Mark knows a lot about leading from the front. It is fitting that in initial media reports of the crash, it was Mark who first reported the famous "Brace for impact" command of Captain Sullenberger and the tone in which he delivered it: "Had he let any tension into his voice it would have been magnified in the passengers." Mark knows about giving firm, calm commands. He was a Marine Corps officer in Operation Desert Storm.

Through our many talks and e-mails since I first reached out to him with the idea of writing a book about Flight 1549 passengers just four days after the crash, I also know Mark as a man of deep faith. He is someone who believes that faith is something that grows, as is goodness, courage, and commitment to living a righteous life. Faith and a soldier's heart are a powerful combination. It has been noted by many that the military training of Captain Sullenberger and some of the men on board helped create a safe and calm movement through this crisis. It has also been clear that faith, for the many who have it, was a cornerstone of this experience.

Mark also believes in heroes, those whose deeds, words, and choices sustain and guide us through any crisis or storm. In his story you will hear about one such hero who just may have inspired the many acts of courage and self-lessness among the passengers. Had those passengers not responded as they did after the plane hit the water, we all might have seen a very different outcome. Held by faith, guided by heroes. As you follow Mark's account, you may choose to reflect on how those same forces may have helped shape you in growing up or enabled you to weather your own storms. And today, perhaps, they can inspire you to become more of who you want to be.

—Kevin

In Mark's Words

PEOPLE OFTEN ASK ME: what was it like to be in that plane when you heard Captain Sully Sullenberger say, "Brace for impact," and you believed you were going to die? The best way I know how to describe it is being enveloped by a deep, peaceful silence, interrupted only by the flight attendants' instructions: "Brace. Brace. Heads down. Stay down." As a person of faith, I sincerely believe that most of us facing our final moments were choosing to pray. As I closed my eyes, my own fast, jumbled prayer sounded something like this:

God, protect and give comfort to my wife, Lisa. Help her find happiness. Give my daughter, Maggie, the strength to stick to her dream of going to NYU and not be haunted by these memories of New York. Help my son, Hayward, get through my loss better than I got through the loss of my brother when I was a teenager. Give comfort to all the passengers and their families. . . . Lord, I don't really want to go like this, but if it's my time, then thy will be done. Thank you for the life I have lived.

I was ready to die because of the assurance that I would meet my Maker. This gives me great comfort and strength. But that wasn't always so. I had seen death up-close before, and the first time challenged my faith. I was a sophomore at The Citadel, following in the footsteps of my older brother Jim, when I received a phone call from my brother-in-law. "Mark, Jim has been in an accident on the interstate," he said. "A drunk driver jumped the median and hit him head-on. He's in the hospital. . . . He needs you."

I prayed to God to spare my brother, but Jim never regained consciousness. I wondered if I would ever regain my faith. "God, how could you take Jim away?" I prayed one night. In my anger and confusion, I tried to become the best pugilist in Charleston, South Carolina, and I was well on my way until the night I fled from the cops after a bar fight I had triggered. If they caught me and pressed charges, I would have been kicked out of school and wound up . . . who knows where?

Our car had just made it through the gates of The Citadel when the cops were intercepted by Colonel Dick, commandant of cadets enforcing student discipline. He didn't let the cops in, and I was not tossed out of school. Years later, at our twentieth class reunion, I asked him why. "Son, you were hurting enough already," he said as he placed his right arm on my shoulder. "Looks like you turned out all right after all."

If I have, I owe it to the trust of Colonel Dick and the faith in God that I finally rediscovered. I needed all of that faith to make it through the sand and the smoke and the stench of death during Desert Storm, while my pregnant wife, Lisa, was back home. I needed it more that day I was approached by my company commander with news. "Lieutenant Hood, give me all your weapons," he ordered. "Your wife is dead, and so are your two children."

Only after hours of anguish, the worst hours of my life, did I learn that this pronouncement was in error: Lisa was very much alive. When I made it home for the premature delivery of our twins Maggie and Hayward, we clung to our faith for weeks as they both fought for their lives. And made it. . . .

Back in those final seconds in the cabin, my training as a Marine Corps officer guided me. I opened my eyes and scanned in all directions. *Contingencies,* I reminded myself. *Think through your contingencies. What will you do if . . . ? Where were all the exits? Who around me might need help, just in case?* I shot one glance out the window to my left. We were gliding just above the water, like a carefree bird! Maybe—bomp, whoosh! When I saw that video of the crash, I was amazed to learn how far the Airbus had skidded and how violent the landing felt to the passengers in the rear. To me, it was like the end of a log ride at an amusement park, when your kids get just jolted enough and just wet enough to have a good time. Only this ride was the start of our renewed life.

Seated in first class, I was one of the first groups of passengers to be escorted out on the port side to the inflated escape chute turned life raft. After gently assisting my seatmate Denise into the raft, I strategically chose a seat toward the rear. Why? It could serve as something of a command post. I could look out for anyone I would need to swim to and get out of the water, and if our life raft didn't hold up, I had a contingency plan for how to keep us all afloat.

We had just entered a critical time, that dangerous interim period when 80 or 90 percent of the greatest danger has passed, but the mission is not yet safely completed. That's when you can lose someone. On a combat mission, it might be someone walking across a minefield after successfully clearing the area of enemy combatants. Here in the icy Hudson, where few passengers had grabbed their flotation device before scrambling out of the plane, it might be someone unable to swim, or panicking, or making an ill-advised choice, or losing strength from hypothermia, or other problems that I couldn't identify but instinctively knew lurked nearby. Surviving this crash landing was too precious a gift to let slip out of our grasp now. It was up to me to use my experience as a leader to assist in any way I possibly could, and with honor. I actually had the thought: *I would rather my corpse be found at the bottom of the Hudson than do anything to dishonor my God, the Marines, or The Citadel.*

My first action here, as it had been in Kuwait, was to pray. Then I made a vow: no one on or near this raft was going down. For a fleeting second, my mind flashed to the memory of fellow Citadel alum Arland D. Williams Jr.

On January 13, 1982, Arland Williams was a passenger on Air Florida Flight 90 out of Washington's National Airport bound for Fort Lauderdale. There was a snowstorm in Washington, and as the NTSB later concluded, the pilot did not take the proper precautions. The plane crashed into the Fourteenth Street Bridge and careened into the ice-covered Potomac River. Of the seventy-nine passengers and crew on board, all but six perished during the crash. The last six initially survived amid the ice chunks in the freezing water where hypothermia was a deadly and immediate threat. It took several minutes before a rescue helicopter could maneuver close enough to extend a lifeline to pull them up, and when the rope was lowered, Arland Williams caught it. But he didn't go up himself. Instead he passed it on to another passenger. Can you imagine such an act of selflessness at that moment? Even more unimaginable is that he did it again, and again, knowing that hypothermia was making it less and less likely he could survive, until all five of the other passengers had been hoisted to safety. When the helicopter returned for Arland Williams, he had perished in the river. That's a hero.

As it turned out, just two days after the twenty-seventh anniversary of the crash into the icy Potomac River, none of us were called to make that supreme sacrifice. We all did our part; we all made it. From my command post, I spotted a couple of passengers swimming dangerously away from the plane and screamed for them to come to our raft, then pulled them in. The woman's lips were blue from hypothermia. I would get to know them as Steve and Pam, and weeks later, during some rough days at work in the slow economy, their expressions of gratitude to me lifted my spirits and kept me stoked for weeks.

But I don't believe I did anything heroic or different from anybody else. You can list countless acts of selflessness among our passengers. Don Norton got that side exit door open immediately. Brad Wentzell cleared a path to get Tess and her baby out of the water-filled rear of the cabin. Dave Sanderson anchored things as one of the last ones out of the back, then stood in waist-deep water until the rescue boat came. Several folks guided eighty-five-year-old Lucille Palmer through the plane and onto the ferry. Others pulled one another out of the water when someone fell off those slippery wings. I like to think that anyone would have reacted in exactly the same way we all did: in the spirit of faith and honor.

I flew home on the next flight back to Charlotte that night. After a few sleep-disturbed nights, I got back to a more even keel in keeping up with my work as a national sales manager. I credit my faith for sustaining me and then guiding me to begin speaking about Flight 1549. I've spoken to churches, large and small, to classes of cadets at The Citadel, to a gathering at Joe Gibbs Racing. I intersperse images from the Hudson with Bible verses and show how God's hand was with us at every turn. I remind audiences that life is fleeting—any breath we take can be the last breath we inhale.

I'm not sure what will come next. Life all around me is changing. Maggie and Hayward just started college, Maggie fulfilling her dream to enroll at NYU, and Hayward earning an Army scholarship and his dad's pride at Virginia Military Institute. As part of my graduation present to them, I wrote them letters in which I included this Biblical passage: ". . . when someone has been given much, much will be required in return" (Luke 12:48). I apply the same message to myself. I can't be sure of God's plan, though I have wondered if it might involve helping in third world countries. Through our church I have been engaged in assistance programs in Rwanda, and I have recently been exploring potential programs of steering medical donor companies in emerging countries and training indigenous peoples.

For our twenty-fourth anniversary, Lisa surprised me with a framed copy of that sketch by *The Sacramento Bee* cartoonist Rex Babin, showing God's hands cradling the wings of our plane in the Hudson. That is the image that I hold in my mind, the image that I pray will continue to guide my choices. No matter what I do, I expect I will continue to share what I believe the Miracle on the Hudson *really* means. Not just for me and my loved ones, and for all my fellow passengers and their families, but for each and every one of us. One way or another, we were all on board this flight together.

P.S. To learn more about the overwhelming response to The Sacramento Bee *cartoonist Rex Babin's illustration of the miracle, see Chapter 26.*

10
Scott Koen:
BEING THERE

*Vision without action is a dream. Action without
vision is simply passing the time. Action with Vision
is making a positive difference.*

—Joel Barker

*Scott spends a lot of his time on the Hudson River on his
forty-six-foot utility boat M/V Lt. Michael P. Murphy. Scott
Koen is one of the rescuers of Flight 1549, and it was quite
an experience traveling the Hudson with him, straight out
to the crash site. Though I visited with Scott months after
the crash, the water was still cold. Hard to even imagine
how cold it was on January 15, 2009. And Scott is quite a
man, with a very deep and rich perspective on life, a long
resume, and a strong sense of his own life's purpose.*

*Scott has saved nine people on this small stretch of the
Hudson River, less than one square mile. Most of his adult
life has been spent here, working first on the Intrepid, a
World War II aircraft carrier turned into a floating
museum, and now on his own boat, which in itself is a
story worth telling. Scott saved his first three people while*

working at the Intrepid, as different circumstances landed three different people in the cold Hudson River. Once, Scott dove in after a woman. Another time, he pulled one up on his smaller boat. A third time, one of his crew fell in. And on January 15, as a private boat that was part of the rescue, Scott saved six more, pulling them up one by one onto the cargo net and into a waiting ferry. For this act of heroism, Scott has received several medals, including the Coast Guard Meritorious Public Service Award given to him by the Secretary of Homeland Security. And he's been honored, along with other New Jersey rescuers, by the New Jersey State Senate and Assembly.

But Scott would not want to be called a hero. He knows who the heroes are, and he has a deep respect for them. His boat is named after one of them: Lt. Michael P. Murphy, Navy SEAL, killed in Afghanistan while radioing in for help for his men. Lieutenant Murphy put himself clearly in harm's way to get that radio call out. He received the Medal of Honor posthumously, the first awarded since the Vietnam War. That's a hero. A book about Lieutenant Murphy and the firefight that killed all but one of his men sits on the dashboard of Scott's boat: Lone Survivor. And after the M/V Lt. Michael P. Murphy, captained by Scott Koen, rushed to the scene of the downed plane, Michael Murphy's father wrote, "It does not surprise me, not only that the MV Lt. Michael P. Murphy would, soon after its christening, be involved in assisting and aiding people in need and danger, but that the person who carries Michael's name on his ship would exhibit those same qualities that made

Navy SEAL Lt. Michael P. Murphy such a special person."

*There are other men and women who are heroes to Scott,
and he honors them as well. But as for himself, Scott would
say, it is the hand of destiny that sometimes puts him in the
right place at the right time.*

—Dorothy

In Scott's Words

I DIDN'T KNOW MICHAEL MURPHY, but I knew of him, and he's
the kind of man that I wanted to carry on my boat. He gave
his life for others, and he did it bravely and calmly. I'm proud
to be carrying on, in whatever way I can, that tradition of
serving. I knew when I got this boat that it would be named
for a hero. I don't take things for granted, and so I want to
make meaning in life, in big things, like naming a boat and
in everyday moments.

I got this boat on eBay. It was a bidding war, but I won and
still the price was a good one. But I got it because it was the
boat I'd used when I worked for the Intrepid Sea, Air & Space
Museum, which floats on the Hudson, right across from where
my boat is berthed. And when I was at the museum, no one
else could fix this boat, a buoy-tender, so a year after I left that
job, the boat also left, and sure enough, she showed up on eBay,
and I bought her. Took a bit of work to get her in shape again,
but I'm mechanically inclined, so I did that. The wife was none
too pleased at first, though after she'd taken a few day trips on

the river and had put her hand to making the boat more homey, she was happy. By the time January 15 came around, she knew for sure that I bought this boat for a good purpose.

And that's pretty much what my life is about. There's always something guiding me. I felt it that day. Bigger hands than mine guided this boat to the rescue. I just happened to be at the marina, shutting the boat up because it was getting so cold. Then the call came in: *Plane ditched in North River.* I was thinking to myself: *Cessna, small plane down. Hope they're okay.* I turned north, not knowing exactly where the downed plane was or how easy it would be to find it. But there was the tail wing, sitting high in the river. Amazing. A jet in the river! I got there quickly, after a few ferries had arrived, and because my boat is low to the water and easy to maneuver, I got in close and began helping with the rescue. One guy, he's a hero, was on the wing in waist-deep water, trying to keep the raft from floating away, holding on to the raft and the emergency exit. He was not even trying to get on the raft, just protecting the fourteen people who were already on it. He was *not* trying to help himself up, but he was freezing and beginning to shake, so I went to help him, and other passengers kept saying, "Take him, take him first!" They'd all seen his willingness to sacrifice, and they wanted him safe. No one was thinking *Me first.* His first words, after thanks, were *Please help the others!* I got him onto my boat and then started helping others up the net. I got six up from where I was. As I pulled the last person up, I lost my glasses, watched them drop. Small price to pay.

My dad was in the military—a pilot—but we grew up way

north in New York and on the water, so I've been around
water my whole life. After Dad retired, he worked for a private company, flying cargo, and he'd sometimes come and
buzz the house and once the school, causing everyone to be
pretty surprised. One day we were out fishing in the middle
of nowhere and a water plane came in for a landing right next
to us. The pilot told us he was lost. So in this whole wide
world and in this huge Adirondacks lake-filled fishing region,
who should he set down next to but a pilot and local air con-
troller, who not only knew exactly how to get this pilot back
on course but showed him the charts and the headings and
got him safely on his way? What are the chances?

I love water. I've always loved water. It's my sign. I worked
on the Intrepid, first as a volunteer and then as an employee
and then up to Director of Operations. I met my wife on the
Intrepid. Now that was being in the right place at the right
time! She was catering an event. We've been happily married
now for twelve years.

I never served in the military, but I do serve, whenever and
however I can. I always want to do for them what they do for us.
They're heroes. I'm a firefighter and when 9/11 happened I was
pretty shaken up—not just because I worked in the city and saw
the damage, but because I knew how many heroes went down
that day. As the city planned a memorial, I added my own plan.
Spent days in my workshop creating a memorial. It was an eagle,
with the names of each person surrounding it. It didn't get cho-
sen. There were so many great ideas, but I never let go of the
thought that I would somehow contribute to healing this event.

In the middle of the night, I got the idea. Use the steel from the Twin Towers as the hull of a new boat for the Navy. I told my boss at the Intrepid, and he loved it. He went to the Navy, and they loved it. I figured out how to get the twenty-four tons of steel that had been salvaged, and slowly but surely the USS *New York* is being built and will be sea-born again. It's like the phoenix rising from the ashes, and it will always represent those 3,000 people who lost their lives. The ship's motto is "Never Forget." There's one strange thing, but I believe all of this fits into a plan: The first USS *New York* had its keel laid on Sept. 11, 1911!

I don't need credit for things like this. By the time something this big is rolling along, I'm one of the little guys. But that's not the point. There's something about energy that I really believe in. Good energy and positivity creates more of that. Good work creates more good. There's a little of me in a lot of places because I carve, in wood and steel, and some of the things I've made—models of the *Intrepid*; a carving from Hull steel with "43" on it, for George Bush, Jr.; and other art memorabilia honoring the military, 9/11, the heroes, and the boats have found their way into the hands of presidents and heads of state and plain folks as well. That's energy. Sometimes it has a form, like one of the pieces of art. Sometimes it is just energy. Either way, it has a positive effect on the world, I believe, and of course on the giver . . . in this case me.

I'm a spiritual person, I guess you'd say, but not religious. I believe in karma and in doing the right thing. There have always been hands (bigger than mine) guiding me. Knowing about Lieutenant Murphy and his men and talking to the aunt of one of the men who went in to save Michael Murphy's team makes me feel humble. I'm a very emotional and open guy. A few weeks after the crash I took a news guy (Chris Cuomo) out on the boat, and he gave his report from the deck. He ended it by saying, "The lieutenant was called to duty one more time . . . and he helped save lives that day." I was so moved by that and it is true. It was my boat and me at the helm, but Lieutenant Murphy's spirit was guiding me.

I can honestly say that nothing bad has ever happened to me in my life. If you can draw a good lesson from a bad event, then it's not bad. Life always turns to crap from time to time, but it's what you do with it that makes it bad or not. I had a good friend who died young. To deal with that I figured out what I liked so much about him, and I became more like him. This is how I carried him and how I learned from the sadness of that experience. Whenever there's something difficult, I try to work through it by doing something positive. If good energy flows through you and you share it, it's a windfall. My theory is that sooner or later irritating things go away. For me it's about being a free spirit, which I am. I do a lot of things from boats to building to art to firefighting. I'm an EMT, a scuba diver, a firefighter, a marine salvage expert. And more. But there's a reason for all that. I'm the only person I know who reads books on survival in the water, how to fly jets, what to do to ditch a plane, medical books. It's not normal. But it's normal for me. I like that stuff and the information, and it keeps me ready, for whatever. My boat is ready for any kind of rescue; my car has a medical kit in it. You never know when you need to be ready, and so many people aren't when a situation arises.

I was ready on January 15. And I was there. What are the chances? Literally ten minutes earlier or later and I wouldn't have been involved. But it's not luck or coincidence. It's destiny. I used to be a survivalist, figuring out how to save myself if the world got crazy, but now if my world comes down I want to be there with it. That's why I'm ready, just to see what those hands are piloting me toward. I don't think the big one has happened—for me, that is. Something bigger is going to happen. I always knew that. For some reason it's my destiny, and I'm not done yet. When jets fall out of the sky and land in front of me, there's a reason for that.

I'm taking this experience back into life as a way to be more of the man I always want to be. I'm partly trying to pull together some amazing things, on big and little scales, so I pay attention to opportunities, and I think about actions or events or creations that would be meaningful. At the same time I am patient, knowing that something is out there waiting for me. The hand of fate will grab me again. When it does, I hope it will be to help other human beings, to remember heroes, to do a good deed. It's all about the energy. I'm glad to be alive, and I'm even more to glad to have helped other people be alive. Let's see what's waiting around the corner.

REFLECTIONS

> *The invariable mark of wisdom is to see the miraculous in the common.*
>
> —Ralph Waldo Emerson

The water landing of Flight 1549 was not common. By all accounts, it was a miracle. A miracle born of many things: the pilot and crew, trained and prepared; the passengers, alert and responsive; the rescuers, helping at every turn; and some fortunate circumstances—good weather, a clear stretch of water, the time of day. Everyone survived. There can be nothing but good feelings about this miracle. But finally, after the crash, the escape from a sinking plane, the rescue and boat rides to the shore, stepping on dry ground, each of our passengers faced the first day of the rest of their lives. It was not, for any of them, just another day. They were now survivors and their lives changed, forever.

Being a survivor, of any disaster or trauma, leaves us with a new set of questions. When bad things happen, we often hear: *Why me?* But when we make it through an ordeal that might well have been our last, we also ask, with an altogether different tone: *Why me?* This heartfelt plea leads us to the biggest and most important questions we can ever ask. And in asking them, and working over a lifetime to answer them, we are living the miracle. *What is my life purpose?* This is the question many passengers started asking after this crash. But it is a question all of us are always asking, whether consciously or not. Life makes sense only when we are connected to a sense of purpose, so we must keep looking for the signs that point us in the right direction. And it is on this path, whatever it is, that miracles await us.

We all know what it is like to feel like we've strayed from the path. We may notice we've been grumpy for a few days and realize this is not who we want to be. It may be a much larger realization that we need to change our lives in some significant way. The call of self or soul or purpose comes to us in many ways and after a crisis—a plane crash, real or metaphoric—we are invited, quite vividly, to pay attention to that call. But the very good news, for all of us, is that we don't need a powerful wake-up call to wake up! Waking up is simply the life's work of paying closer and closer attention to that which is important.

Holding to the widest possible vision of the world, life can be what you make it. We experience ourselves, sometimes, as being no more than a small boat, rudderless, on a big sea, pulled and pushed and sometimes toppled by the winds and water of life. When that happens, as it does to all of us, we are left to draw on resources, inner and outer, to keep that boat afloat. *How do I navigate through this life?* In a crisis, it's a big and urgent question, but every day brings us choice points, large and small. Every choice leads us into an unknown future. And every moment invites us to express our true self.

But how do we get "it"—get what we are being called toward, get answers to our big questions, get guidance on this path of life? Signs that remind us of what is important come in all sizes. The airplane crash is a big sign; the gentle voice inside reminding us to be kind is a smaller sign. Warren managed to create a way to step back from varying moods or reactions into what is important for him, through what he called his circuit breaker. Bill Elkin, thinking he must do something big with his life, realized he needed to be the best father he could be. An annoyance, a judgment, a short temper, self-criticism, inattention, and so many other habitual ways of being can be reconsidered in the light of what we truly value and who we truly are. The signposts are everywhere.

Are we living our faith? Are we listening to our own inner wisdom? Are we being true to ourselves?

Appreciating what we have, rather than what we don't, is one of the ways we awaken to the purpose of our lives. If the grass is always greener on the other side, we are never *here and now,* in the life we are living. The more we check in with our own truth, our values, and our own deepest desires, the more we will live a life that is here and now, and honestly, that's the only life there is! The more we live in tune with what is most important to us, the more peace we will find and share with others. Barry has found that he has many thank-you's to share with the world, and he is doing that. Michele, struggling with her love of family and her desire for independence, struggling with her adventurous spirit now boxed in by a fear of flying, has discovered interdependence: the best of both worlds.

The life we live will be our legacy. The miracle is in every step we take. When we wake up, even a bit, to a deeper way of knowing, we will be better people: a goal that each of our passengers has felt deeply called to. *How shall I live this life?* That is what we keep asking. And there are so many ways to live this life. For these people, every one has deepened their love of family and friends, renewed their respect for heroes and mentors, and committed themselves to honoring the miracle that is their life. Each of us can do that as well.

Part III
A Time to Learn,
A Time to Heal

To every thing there is a season, and a time to every purpose under the heaven.

—Ecclesiastes 3:1

11
Brad Wentzell:
SOMETHING GOOD

Power is the ability to do good things for others.

—Brooke Astor

Like so many passengers from Flight 1549, Brad lives in
Charlotte. But to friends, colleagues, and the guys at the
gym, he is known as "Boston." He grew up north of Boston
in Atkinson, New Hampshire, with the Massachusetts bor-
der at the end of the road he lived on. He and his childhood
friends would take turns jumping back and forth over the
imaginary line and shouting, "I'm in Massachusetts now!
I'm in New Hampshire now!" A high school wrestler, Brad
passionately followed the Boston pro-sports teams, especially the New England Patriots. After his family moved to
Charlotte prior to his junior year in high school, he was
not even remotely tempted to switch pro football allegiances
to the Charlotte-based Carolina Panthers. Loyalty to his
hometown team was much too strong. He decorated his
home office in Patriots' blue and searched for weeks to find
a car just that color. As you read Brad's story, you will learn
just how important loyalty remains to him today.

During our interview, Brad freely admits that many of

his childhood memories are not happy ones. In school he routinely found himself forced to sit facing the wall, or plunked in the hallway during class, or held inside during recess for some kind of trouble. Grades were a struggle, and he was eventually diagnosed with both ADD and hyper-activity. "I was like a shaken-up Coke can ready to explode," he explains. "My mother fought tooth and nail with the teachers on my behalf, and after I'd come home from a bad day at school, she would just hold me and say, 'Shhh, it's okay, sweetie. Don't worry.' That helped." Brad knew he wasn't really a bad kid, but labels have a way of stinging—and sticking. The tag has not prevented him from succeeding in business as an adult. At thirty-two, he handles major responsibilities as an East Coast Regional Manager and vendor for a prominent national company. But those childhood memories, and the echoes ("Bad kid, bad kid!"), would sometimes ring in his ears. Then, after his experience on January 15 and in the pivotal days and weeks that followed, the echoes were met with a very different and more powerful refrain. Flight 1549, and how Brad acted in the middle of it, had changed the script. Brad recognized the clear and compelling needs of others around him and responded in a way that may well have saved lives! So now those new echoes ("hero" or "great man") continue to fill his days and nights, and he doesn't expect them to be going away any time soon. For that, he is resoundingly grateful. Perhaps his story may lead us to wonder how and where we might heed a call to action today in our lives, to

*do something good that can quiet any of those painful or
limiting echoes we may carry.*

— Kevin

In Brad's Words

My dad and I are best friends. He's my hero. Before the flight
that day, we were on the phone "arguing" about whose house we
would be at for the Super Bowl party in a couple of weeks. He
told me, "No way I'm coming to your house. Last time I did that
the Patriots were 18–0 and they lost the Super Bowl to the Giants.
Your place is bad luck!" We were still kidding about it when I had
to put away my cell for the flight. After we made it out of the
plane, I immediately called my wife. I knew how worried she
would be! I told her I was in a plane crash and was in the Hudson
River and to notify my family that I was alive. Later, from the
back of the raft, I called my dad back. He saw my number on his
phone, but he hadn't heard the news. So his first words were to
me were, "Brad, I'm still not coming to your house for the Super
Bowl. I've got to let you go. I'm busy and need to call you back!"

I said, "Dad, you're not going to let me go. I'm in the Hudson
River, my plane crashed, and I'm so cold."

He knew I was serious then. It was good to hear his voice.
When things were much calmer a while later, I called him
again and as soon as he picked up the phone I said, "And you
are coming to my house for the Super Bowl." That was my way
of sending a signal that I was okay.

A few weeks after the crash, it was my dad who really got me thinking about all the media attention. That day, when a group of us got on the next flight home to Charlotte after the crash, I was interviewed on TV with my Red Cross blanket on saying, "This guy [Sully Sullenberger] is the reason my two-and-a-half-year-old daughter still has a dad and my wife still has a husband." I travel from Maine to South Carolina for my work, and it seemed like everywhere I went, every hotel TV I would turn on, I would hear that sound bite over and over. A guy at my gym near Charlotte was tying his shoe near me one day and he said, "I heard that bad accent on TV and I looked closely and sure enough, there's your mug up there." I had been on CNN with Larry King and Wolf Blitzer, and even on *Dr. Phil*. It was a wild experience for a guy who sells doors.

That's when Dad said, "You've got to Google yourself." So I did, and I saw thousands of pages with my name on it. It wasn't just that sound bite. It was about what happened to me and other people around me on the plane and what I did. . . . I'm not comfortable with the term *hero*. I've been an imperfect person, for sure, and I come from a family of cops and firefighters and a father who was a Vietnam combat veteran. The kinds of things I did on that plane, they do every day. It was something anyone would have done, really.

Here's how it started:

> *I'm seated in 21C, near the back. When we're going down, I say the Lord's Prayer, and then I add, "Lord, I have not lived the perfect life. Forgive me for my sins. Take care of my wife and daughter." They're telling us to brace, but I*

*think: I'm about to die. I'm not spending my last moments
with my head in my crotch. So I sit up to get one last
glimpse of God's earth, and all of a sudden I have the most
calming moment of my life. My comfort zone in life is the
smell of my daughter, Kaylee—bath, pee-pee diapers, night
sweat, baby powder. To a dad, it combines for a very sweet
smell. And as I watch those last seconds I can smell my
daughter, and it's so soothing, even as I wait for the plane
to be ripped into pieces.*

*Then, when we crash and the plane does get ripped
underneath and the water is flooding in fast, I feel so clear
and so focused. I believe my ADD was a gift from God
because even when I was young I could focus on some very
specific things in front of me, and in that moment I just
seem to know exactly what's going on around me. I had
never been so focused in my life. And I can see that we have
to get out of there fast and that some people are not so
focused. So I fly into action. I grab one older man's shirt
and say, "Get up! Come on. Go!" To the others I shout,
"Move! Move! Don't reach for any of your stuff—whatever
you're reaching for, someone is going to drown because of
it." I feel like a drill sergeant. "Go! Go! Keep walking!
Keep moving!"*

*So we're all moving forward, and I can see the exit by
the wing, and I really want to get off that damn plane and
get home. I'm thinking, Life is right here in front of me. I
can get out alive. But then I hear a woman and her baby
screaming, and I look back and I see her clutching her baby.*

The water is waist deep, the aisle is blocked, and she's try-
ing to climb over the seats holding her baby and she's . . .
sort of trapped. They both look scared to death. I say to
myself, "If you don't go back and help her, you'll never for-
give yourself." So I push one guy out of the way, and I get
to them, and I just bear-hug her and the baby and say,
"Come on, you're coming with me. Let's go!" I'm yelling at
the others to keep moving and they're listening, maybe
because I'm a pretty big guy—about 215 pounds and I can
bench press 370 pounds. I get them all the way to the exit,
and I hand the baby to someone else. They're gonna make
it now, I think.

On the wing we all can see that the life raft won't stay up,
and no one can get on it. It's like when you're a kid and you
can't get on a float in the deep water because all the weight
is on one end and when you try to get on, it just keeps tip-
ping. So Carl, this guy I have been talking to on the wing,
tells me someone is going to have to get that raft up. "Kid,
you have to go in," he says. "Give me your hand. I've got
you. Don't worry." I look at him, knowing I outweigh this
guy by a lot, and I say, "Carl, are you going to be able to
hold me?" He looks at me with a very serious look. "I've
got you—trust me!" he says, and so I do. He's got me by
the wrist. So I leap in, water up to my chest, and I grab on
to the strap and pull myself into the back of the raft. That's
what it needed, some weight in the back. So I stay in the
back of the raft, and everyone is able to get on.

While I'm in the raft, a gentleman slips off the wing. Carl and I and other passengers grab him by the pants, and he's definitely suffering from hypothermia. We wind up pushing him up the Jacob's ladder onto the ferry, just muscling him up. He was a big guy. On the ferry we stay with him, get him to the back, try to get him moving. Slowly he comes around. He makes it.

So that was my experience on Flight 1549. After I got home on the later flight to Charlotte that night and finally got to bed, my mind was playing tricks on me in my sleep. I convinced myself in one of my dreams that I didn't wake up, that I really didn't make it. Then my daughter—I need to tell you that we have this joke: I always tickle her, and she says, "Dada, you funny." So when I was having that dream I felt her hand reach over and rub the scruff of my face. All of a sudden I woke up, though I was still kind of dazed. I looked up at the ceiling and I asked: *Am I really here?* But I saw her sweet face, and the words tumbled out: "You have no idea what happened to me yesterday, do you?" And she said, "Dada, you funny." There was my little girl, and right beside her my wife—my friend, my companion, my beloved. In that moment I realized I was alive.

The next day I stopped by my mother's workplace unannounced, and when she finally saw me it was like something out of a movie. She held me for a long time: "Shhh, it's okay, don't worry, it's all right." I had not been held like that since I was a child, and for that moment I was a kid again—an oversized kid but a kid nonetheless. And that felt great.

Then all the media started, and I told the story about what I did. I went to my church, Forest Hill in Charlotte, and David Chadwick, the pastor, knew I was there and asked me to stand in my seat, right there with my family. When I stood up, I received a loud standing ovation. That was a first for me, and I had to fight back the tears. I was asked to speak, and I remember saying, "Whatever you may be doing in your life that's bad, stop it." I received a thank-you note from Tess, the mom, which really touched me. When I went on *Dr. Phil* with my wife, Stephanie, the looks I got when he told the audience what I had done were just amazing. It felt like such an out-pouring of respect, appreciation, caring, whatever it was.

And I got to thinking about growing up. When I was young, I wasn't doing all the things I had dreamed of. I didn't get to play much football because I was too busy getting in trouble. I was a failed athlete, I had ADD, and I had led a really wild life. I had done things I was definitely not proud of. But now I thought: *If what I did on the plane was the one moment of really coming through in my life, I'll take it.* After all the bad things I had done, I was able to forgive myself. I had closure.

And in forgiving myself, I was able to begin to let go of anger and grudges I held toward others. It wasn't just from childhood, either. I remember how before the crash I was angry at people around me. This was just after the election, and no matter whether you supported Obama or not, I was just angry about the racism I encountered. You could taste it in the air. The left hated the right and the right hated the left.

We were divided. Now I'm not so angry. I have this newfound faith in humanity. It's come from how so many people have told me, "We're glad you're alive," even people I thought I had burned bridges with when I was young. It's come from the reactions I've seen in my travels for work, at home, all around. It's just how everyone reacted to what happened with Flight 1549. Something really good happened that day, something we needed as a country, and I'm just ecstatic to be a part of it.

As the months have gone by since the crash, I've been thinking about something my uncle Rob said when he was dying of cancer years ago: "The key to life is loyalty, whether it's loyalty toward your family, your religion, your work, your sports teams—everything comes down to loyalty." I believe it was loyalty that helped us all do the right thing at the crash. We were loyal to one another and to the cause of everyone getting out alive, and no one was left behind.

When I was in third grade I discovered a poem I liked: "Success." I put a copy of it in my pocket, and later in life I kept it in my wallet and even read it at my wedding. I remember the lines about "to laugh often and much" and "to leave the world a bit better." It ends with:

> To know even one life has breathed
> Easier because you have lived;
> This is to have succeeded.

It just seemed to fit how I felt about what I had done. Maybe it fit the whole picture of Flight 1549. I used to wonder sometimes if I was a coward, but now I know, for the rest of my life, I'm not a coward. I was tested, and apparently I passed the test.

It's September now. I'm getting ready for the start of the Patriots season on the Monday Night Football game with my brother Ricky, who is my other best friend. I'm taking a personal day from work. I'll put my new team jersey on over the lucky T-shirt I wore for all three of their Super Bowl championships. I'll have my two-day Tom Brady beard. My dog, Guido, wearing his own Patriots jersey, will be to my left, and my lucky beer chiller will be to my right. The Patriots flag will be outside my door, flying an hour before the game, and I will be holding my lucky football. I'll be ready to do my share. The new year will begin, and it will be sweeter because I'm here for it and because I now know there are so many good people in this world. And that last winter, just before the Super Bowl, maybe I had done something good, too.

12
Maryann Bruce:
BEING THE SURVIVOR

Fall seven times, stand up eight.

—Japanese proverb

Maryann Bruce has an unusual story. The Hudson River plane crash was not her first brush with death, nor was it her second. She has skated through seven real or potential disasters. Can you imagine? Seven times coming close to a tragedy or disaster and seven times escaping. Clearly this is one determined woman, something I glimpse as I await our meeting. First, she didn't hesitate to take the only interview slot I could offer, though it meant an extremely early drive from her home well north of Charlotte. Now, thirty minutes before our scheduled interview, it is absolutely pouring. She calls and apologizes: the highways are backed up and she will be a bit late. Many others would have turned around and headed home, but such an act would not fit Maryann's personality or approach to unforeseen problems of any stripe. She will persevere.

In the interview, we cover all the details of Maryann's Seven Lives. "This is the most thorough interview I've had about all this," she observes. I take it as a compliment, but *mostly I'm just fascinated. Beyond the who-what-when-where-why of Maryann's near-death adventures, I learn some things I had not expected: Before Flight 1549 she was not always so cool, calm, and confident during these potential disasters. And she didn't always walk away from the rubble with a "you'll never get me" wave of the hand.*

Somehow this makes her portrait as "The Survivor" more human, more complete. We can learn from her about being the survivor and apply it to our own lives because we can connect with her fearlessness and her fear. We can then look through our own experiences and remind ourselves that we also have survived "something," maybe more than one something, even if our dangerous moment did not make Headline News. And no matter how royally or how feebly we think we may have handled it, somehow we got through. Knowing that can help us tap into the will to go on living without fear. Maybe even with a little flair.

—Kevin

In Maryann's Words

PEOPLE WHO DON'T KNOW ME often assume that I must have bad associations with airplanes. I have to set them straight. First of all, I survived that plane crash in the Hudson, and it was just my Seventh Life anyway. I must have two more coming to me, right? But it's more than that. Planes to me, despite more than one harrowing adventure in the air, will always have a happy connotation. Trust me on this.

To explain, I have to go back to late 1981. I was a senior at Duke University, and if you are a student at Duke you have to be a serious Blue Devils basketball fan. I had been home in Long Island for a getaway, and I wasn't supposed to return to campus until Sunday night, but there was a big game on Sunday and I wanted to be there. So I was flying standby out of LaGuardia on Saturday night, and when I got on the packed flight, I found the overhead bins full. Looking for anyplace to put my suitcase, I noticed a sportscoat with nothing on top or below it.

"Excuse me, whose is this?" I asked the nearby passengers as I held up the coat. When a young man answered, "Oh, that's mine," I asked him, "Would you mind if I put my suitcase under it?"

He politely responded, "That would be fine."

"Oh my God, you're from Britain!" I said with a grin.

"And you're from the Bronx!" he shot back. Well, he was close.

I guess he thought I was attractive with my dark hair and heels, and you can say I noticed him too. We talked for most of the flight to Raleigh-Durham, with me in an aisle seat and he in the middle seat behind me. When the plane landed, Ron told me he lived in Raleigh and handed me his card, so of course I gave him my number because girls didn't call guys. "If a guy with a British accent calls, find me," I instructed my roommate. "I met the man I'm going to marry on the plane!" He did call, we were engaged by Valentine's Day, and we've

been married for more than twenty-five years, a milestone
linked to the Hudson, because I had taken off the diamond
ring he had given me for our anniversary before that flight,
and it got swept away with the rest of my belongings.

Still, my good feelings about airplanes did not get washed
down the Hudson that day. I've been flying regularly for my
work as president of a New York investment firm ever since.
I even flew recently to Hawaii, site of my first against-all-odds
experience. Okay, this one barely counts. Ron and I were
enjoying our first vacation as a married couple, lounging
poolside at the Turtle Bay Hilton in Oahu, when sirens went
off and a local blurted out, "Tsunami! Evacuate to higher
ground!" They took us to a church but when they let us back
we learned the big tsunami had been a dud. As an associate
on my recent Hawaii visit recalled, "Oh, that was the six-inch
tsunami."

My Second Life was September 1985, surviving Hurricane
Gloria—in an airplane. Our flight from Nashville to New
York cut through the teeth of the hurricane that raced up the
East Coast and made its second landing on Long Island,
something we discovered only later when we saw the
uprooted trees and roofs ripped off houses. But my memories
of Gloria focus more on what happened *before* the hurricane.
Ron and I came to be on that flight only because, while we
were in Chicago for the funeral of the best man from our
wedding, I got a call that my father had suffered a heart attack
and might be close to death. We quickly drove off toward our
home in Nashville, but on the way, somewhere in Indiana, in

the dead of night, our car broke down. In this snapshot, you won't see me scoffing at danger. I was a crying mess.

"Will someone please come?" I begged.

A man tapped on our windshield. Not just a man—a priest. I bawled out our story, and after listening intently he said simply, "I will help." He took us to his home and a few phone calls later this priest had four parishioners around our car, led by the local Cadillac dealer supervising our repairs. They got us safely back on the road, we made our Gloria-destined flight at the last minute, and Dad survived that heart attack. I never saw the priest again. I'm not religious per se, but I do believe I had a guardian angel looking after me that day.

My next life? Another easy one. In 1987, Ron and I had enjoyed a day of skiing at Breckenridge, a popular Colorado resort. When we got back to our hotel, I flipped on the news and saw a strange sight: the side of the mountain we had skied on just hours earlier was buried in an avalanche! Just good timing, I guess.

Flash forward to February 26, 1993. The World Trade Center. Bad timing for all of us there. When the South Tower shook violently, my first thought was a small prop plane had struck the side of the building: an accident. We all rushed to the windows, but there wasn't much to see. So we went back to work until my secretary came back from the ladies' room reporting smoke. Time to evacuate.

We banded together to head down thirty-plus flights of stairs in the pitch black and swirling smoke. We even set up a team of six young guys to take turns carrying our female employee in a body cast from a skiing accident. I can vividly recall how we all counted stairs: twelve one floor, thirteen the next, twelve, thirteen, twelve, thirteen. I hopped a cab to Penn Station and a train to Long Island, and when I got home Ron looked more shaken than I did.

"Didn't you know?" he said. "There was a terrorist attack." No, I didn't know, but I soon learned that the terrorists had actually meant to take both towers down.

Less than a year later I had flown from my home in Charlotte to Los Angeles for business. No problems on this flight, but when I stepped into the cab at LAX and told my cabby where to take me, he turned around and gave me a strange look.

"Don't you know?" he asked. "We just had an earthquake early this morning." No, actually, I never seem to know about these things until later. Maybe I should have a meter with me at all times: Disaster Ahead.

"The place you want to go is right near the epicenter. We're not going there!" he commanded. "Where are you staying? I'll take you to your hotel."

As an Easterner, I didn't know my earthquakes, and I wasn't sure if this guy was maybe being a *little* too cautious—until I began seeing chunks of fallen buildings. Okay, I'll stay put. Soon after checking into the airport hotel, I saw the TV scenes of devastation; this was the 6.7 magnitude Northridge Earthquake of 1994. Before long, I wasn't just watching—my hotel room walls were rattling and whatever they had hanging there came tumbling down from aftershock upon aftershock.

"I want to get out of here—now!" I told my airline. "Sorry, no flights available until morning," the agent responded. *I have to spend all night riding the aftershocks of a California earthquake?*

"Why are all these things happening to me?" I demanded on the phone with Ron. "The tsunami, the hurricane, the avalanche, the bombing, and now an earthquake?"

Calmly he responded, "You'll be all right. Earthquakes happen all the time in California."

Well, not earthquakes that leave seventy-two dead and nine thousand injured. "But I was younger when those other things happened," I said. "And now I'm . . . "

Five months pregnant with my second child, Vicky, actually. That just might have had something to do with my weepiness. But Vicky was born that May on solid ground, and as I was raising these two great kids, I actually had a quiet stretch there. Until that flight from Charlotte to Boston on the morning of 9/11.

"There's been an accident—a plane has hit the World Trade Center," the pilot announced. "We're going to be detained." I turned to the woman beside me and in tears proclaimed, "No, I was in the Trade Center before, and they swore they would take both buildings down. This is *not* an accident!" Moments later, the news was confirmed. The pilot began a series of conflicting announcements: *We're on a temporary holding pattern. We're going to DC. We're going to be kept waiting in the air indefinitely. We're cleared to land at Logan, but the National Guard will be waiting to escort us.* And while soaring over New York: "If you look down, you can see the smoke."

On our escorted walk past the pubs in Logan, we watched the TV images of both towers going down. I thought of Ron, whom I couldn't reach because the phone lines were jammed. I later learned that he strongly suspected I had been on one of the hijacked planes. Neighbors told me, "If you ever wondered if your husband *really* loves you, don't." I thought of my former colleagues who still worked at the World Trade Center. Did they make it out? Amazingly, they all did. Two days later I got home to Ron, and to more questions: *What were the odds that I would be inside the World Trade Center for the first terrorist attack and then in an airplane during the second attack? Just how many disasters will I run into? Will I get to see my kids finish high school?* Then another voice: "You know, Maryann, somehow you keep surviving these things. Maybe there is another plan. You're a survivor."

Vowing to enjoy a life without fear, I indulged in a round of semiretirement in 2007, during which I experienced what it was actually like to spend time at our wonderful home. I made an astounding discovery: who I am is not defined by what I *do*. I embraced new work and a renewed purpose and passion.

When Sully veered off toward the Hudson, it never dawned on me that I wasn't getting off that plane alive. I was mostly cool and calm except that I was determined that come hell or high water I was going out to the river with my purse—I had to call Ron right away this time so he wouldn't have to worry for hours like he did after 9/11. When I told him I was on the Hudson he said, "No, you can't be on the Hudson, you must be on the East River."

I shot back, "No, I'm on the Hudson. Stop arguing!"

It's funny when we play out our little routine to friends now.

When the media started picking up on my Seven Lives, I played along with the humor, to a point. If someone called me a jinx and asked never to travel with me, I said, "No, I'm a good luck charm. You're with me, nothing bad can happen in the end." Yet from the start I was reminded of the more frightening side of what happened, and what could have happened, on the Hudson. The police officer assisting me during the rescue confided that when he answered the code for this emergency, he expected another 9/11. "Instead, for once, everyone lived," he said. "It's the happiest day of my life."

In some ways, it feels like that happiest day to me, too. I still get to be here for my children, Alexander and Vicky, through new milestones in their lives. Also, wonderful doors keep opening. I heard from my sorority Big Sister at Duke for the first time in ten years. It turns out she has a daughter who was entering Duke with my son, and we got to spend time together catching up on our lives. I can't even recall why we lost touch, but I'm happy to have this chance to rekindle the relationship.

I don't spend much time trying to calculate the odds of surviving all these mishaps. You could never do it. Sometimes I wonder what it is that makes me, or any of us, a survivor. I was recently looking through the book *Deep Survival: Who Lives, Who Dies and Why* by Laurence Gonzales and resonated with some of the survival traits he pointed to: keep your cool and your sense of humor; notice your surroundings; take decisive and appropriate action; believe that you will succeed. They all help, but I don't have the magic answer. Some of it is a mystery. And I know that more of these things will happen, as they will to us all. I'm just clear that I will not live my life afraid of them. In my heart of hearts I feel like I have more to accomplish on this planet.

And maybe I just am that good luck charm. Remember the diamond ring I got for my twenty-fifth anniversary that got left behind on our plane? In June, US Airways delivered it to me in solid condition. Why would I not love flying?

13
Matt Kane:
SEEKING THE SULLY MOMENTS

*On the occasion of every accident that befalls you,
Remember to turn to yourself And inquire what
power you have for turning it to use.*

—Epictetus

By the time I was saying good-bye to businessman Matt
Kane, we'd visited a large world, ranging from the merits of
Derek Jeter to the importance in Matt's life of his mom,
"who was super tough and five foot nuthin'!" Matt has done
a lot with his life, had a lot of success, has a family he loves,
and works hard. And Matt continues to hone the skills that
make him the man he wants to be. Matt didn't have a great
epiphany after his miracle survival . . . and, in fact, I don't
think he'd use the word miracle to describe the amazing
landing. He'd likely compare the process to having a great
athlete at the helm, and a great team on board, each doing
their part to win the game.

Aside from business and family life, Matt's also a martial
artist: a black belt in karate. It's a fighting style. "The goal
is to control the outcome, at the same time knowing you
can't control everything." Matt and I share this experience

of martial arts, and so I got to see into his world through that lens, and it is clear that this intense experience—a fight that demands the best in each person, that is grounded in fairness, strength, and a spiritual perspective—is a good metaphor for Matt's life. Matt's four-year-old son has recently joined him in martial arts training.

"You have to be ready for any punch or kick that comes," he says. *"It's easy to talk yourself out of staying focused. I can't do it. Too much going on. I have no control. But there's always something we can control, something we can work with." That, for Matt, is greatness, not so much the win or loss, not the big score, but being there, fully aware and ready to show up . . . for whatever life brings. He saw this focus, this greatness, in Sully and his crew. "They're the Tiger Woods of pilots," Matt told* ABC News. *"Unbelievable!" Yet for Matt, aiming to be just that is totally believable.*

In Matt, we see strength and vulnerability side by side. He is strong, physically active, clear, and articulate. You'd want him on your side on the team . . . or in the plane. And when he talks about his mom, his eyes tear up.

—Dorothy

In Matt's Words

THE BIGGEST THING FOR ME is seeing the world in a different way. Some of the boundaries or fears that held me back aren't there anymore. I'm trying to do the right thing. Part of what

that means is not being afraid of the elephant in the room—
not being afraid to say what is true or what I see and know.
I've come away with a few deep lessons. The first is "Be
direct," and the second is "Everybody has a Sully Moment."
My job is just to figure out how to react in that moment (and
there are many of them, from the little everyday moments to
the life-and-death issues). There's stuff we can control and
stuff we can't, but we'd better know the difference! If I can do
that, life is not that hard.

Anyone can have a Sully Moment—that moment when you
step up and give it your best shot, moments of readiness in the
face of fear, total commitment even when you can't possibly
know the outcome. It doesn't have to be at the level of Sully
with 155 lives on the line. It can come with any situation, any
moment of time when you are at the crossroads and your
whole life has been preparing you for that moment, and then
you just go for it. I truly believe that people have it in them
and can do this many times, with family or friends, or at work.
But most people sit back and let these Sully Moments go by.
They don't execute it. At work I tell my people, "You will have
these moments with clients, so don't let them pass you by."

The day I passed my test to earn my black belt, I would
call that a Sully Moment. The whole training is a hard physical and mental drain. You train and practice and prepare. I
was in the best shape of my life, cardiovascular and muscular.
But the reality is you're not really tested until that moment
when you take the test, be it an actual test or the test life
throws at you.

A good friend of mine of twenty years had a Sully Moment that showed me how respect, friendship, and honor are much more important than material items. Chris Mezzatesta ("Mezz") and I had worked for a "mom and pop" company that had grown to be the fourth largest paging carrier in the US. It was our first job out of college as sales interns, and over ten years we grew to become the Senior VP and VP of sales. On December 4, 2000, the company declared bankruptcy. We had to tell one thousand sales people and two thousand others their company was no longer. With padlocks going on the door within hours of the announcement, Mezz had assembled a skeleton crew of forty to stay on during liquidation. While negotiating for double pay and stay bonuses with the bankruptcy attorneys and the bank-hired crisis manager, he had the opportunity to better his personal compensation five times. But that would mean the Band of Forty would have to settle for just having a job and receiving their normal pay. Mezz turned this opportunity down without even a thought. The Band of Forty would receive higher wages.

When I asked him about that Sully Moment in the conference room, he had that same look in his eye that I have seen in others. Clarity, focus, and never a doubt of what his actions should be. To this day we respect him for his selflessness, and he is like a brother to me. Mezz has a seat on my plane for life.

There are other Sully Moments that are not as grand and happen to us every day. For example, I play softball on a company team. I want to play my best but not be a showman,

not get the ego involved in that way of showing off or showing someone else up. That's what seems most important to
me. It's easy to turn away, let that ball pass you by for fear of
striking out. It's also easy to be so full of yourself that you
take a wild swing, all ego and pride. Greatness is in the
moment of paying attention and giving it your best shot.
There's always the risk of striking out, but you've got to get
up to the plate and take your shot.

There is a clarity with me now that I didn't have before. I
try, whether it is with work or home or softball, to listen and
see the full picture where I used to only see a partial one. I
recently hired two people for the company, and I saw they
had a skill set that was different from what our company val-
ued at the time. Even though I was met by resistance from my
boss and my boss's boss, I persisted because I knew they
would work well in our company. It takes some time, but it
is really seeing the person, not just the resume, that makes it
clear that he or she is a good fit—or not. I don't know quite
how I do that, but I think these are mini–Sully Moments . . .
really being there to see that person I'm interviewing, to hear
the deeper truth, and to decide. And part of the clarity is that
idea of being direct. In the past if I'd seen someone be disre-
spectful, I would've just turned away. Now I'll say something.
Life is too important to me to turn away from something that
I know is wrong.

I'm really about living as a win-win situation. I don't want
to have any regrets. I don't want to second-guess myself, so I
pay attention. I have to check in with myself to make sure

I'm on track. I've always been self-reflective and am good at taking in feedback. That really helps. Feedback is what your bosses or your teammates or your family say to you. It's also seeing the world around you, seeing what feedback is out there about what's possible, about what will work.

I have twins, four years old: a boy and a girl, Rogan and Alexandra. My wonderful wife, Tracey, and I take a proactive approach with them. We didn't tell them about the crash. We couldn't see how it would help them now. There's a lesson to be learned for them, as there was for me, but they're too young now. We'll tell them when the time is right. I love them so much.

My dad was a marine. We lived in New Jersey in an affluent community, and we weren't at all wealthy. That helped set up some core values. We learned young what's right, what's important. Dad was big on responsibility: team and personal. Play for the team not for your own glory. Take responsibility for whatever is on your plate. They were Irish Catholics, and I've carried their values, though I do it differently. My dad and I barely talked until I was seventeen. That's the way it was in those days. I didn't follow in his footsteps by being in the military, but I did by having his values: focus, no showboating, being singular in pursuit of what's important.

I instill values in my kids, and they are disciplined, well-behaved, and lovely. We have rules and we teach them right from wrong, but we also want them to express themselves. We're much warmer as a family now, lots of hugging, and if one of the kids is scared or just happens to fall asleep on me, I'm happy for that. A year ago, because of my orientation to work, I would have fought the idea of a family day out, but tomorrow we're going to Six Flags, and I'm happy to do so. Twelve hours of having my kids having fun and me having it with them—what could be better? It's the team thing. Family as a team.

My parents are in North Carolina now, and they're very proud of me. Oddly, my older brother was flying the same day on US Airways. And at the rescue site, I found an old fraternity brother. He'd been on the same plane, but I didn't know it. I hadn't seen Jay in fifteen years. Suddenly, this crazy accident opens another door. Here's an old friend, and now he's a friend again. I never want to pass something by that's important. But it's easy to do so, getting caught in life, getting caught in the noise.

During the crash I felt like I moved through three phases. Each was a distinct focus of attention. Breaking it down like that increases the likelihood of survival, I think. If everything comes rushing in—the noise, thoughts, fears, hopes—then focus is lost . . . just like in softball or karate . . . or a day at Six Flags.

For me the focus was:

1) Survive the crash.
2) Get out of the plane alive.
3) Get to a boat.

I was so focused. There is a way to survive . . . at least a way that as a person we have a better chance to do so. But everything I already knew, the lessons I'd learned from my dad and mom, they were all there. It was a team effort. It wasn't just about *me* surviving the crash, getting out of the plane, getting to a boat. It was about all of us doing that. While all of this was happening, I didn't hear lot of noise, if you know what I mean. Not just the absence of plane noise, which was also unusual, but the absence of noise in my head. Not a lot of background, just clear focus. In those moments, but I see it is also true in much less crucial circumstances, I take in a lot of data, seeing what's happening in the plane, gathering information, paying attention, but then immediately filtering: what's important, what's not. In this situation and others, big and little, I am sizing up the situation, and then thinking stops and action kicks in.

If I could describe that experience, it's as if it is all there, everything you need to know and everything you need to have. So how do I want to work with it? I don't think there is any situation in life that is not like this. Everything seems so clear at a moment like this. I don't see what I don't need to see, and I don't hear anything that draws my attention away. This is what I've carried away from this accident. And here's the thought I've had quite a few times since then. When I meet a new person, socially or professionally, pretty quickly I ask the question, *Do they have a seat on my plane?* It's about selfless versus selfish. Do they see the bigger picture? Or do they think they are bigger or more important than someone else? Greatness is not putting yourself first. It's being on the team, playing your part, and doing it well.

Greatness is a word I think about, and it is not the alpha-male thing. If something works at my job, there's a big success. I don't need to take credit. I'd just as soon share that credit around and let everybody shine. But really it's at the end of the day, when I'm checking in on myself that I can figure out a bit how I'm doing. How do I feel about who I've been that day? Was I a good dad, a good teammate? Did I work hard and train hard? Was I kind to a stranger? Did I remember to appreciate the people I love? That's where greatness is.

When the plane was going down, I was scared, no doubt about it, but I also knew, deeply, that my kids and wife would be okay, and I had no regrets. That was a good feeling. I'm thirty-eight, and I have no regrets. I don't know if there's any better way to check in on your life than to see whether there are regrets.

This crash was like living through my own funeral in some ways. I heard from people I hadn't seen in twenty years. People I'd fired called to tell me they were so glad I was alive, to tell me they weren't angry, they'd found new jobs, learned an important lesson, gone on to be better for it. It's like all the feedback I've gotten from people is the best stuff I'd want on my tombstone. "He was a good man!" I hear a lot, "I can't believe how far you've come." I have. I'm happy it's so. I wouldn't trade this experience for anything in the world!

P.S. The miracle lives on: Matt Kane's sister-in-law is expecting a baby boy. It is their first. His name will be Hudson. And Matt just got his kids a puppy named, of course, Sully.

14
Don Norton:
RESPECTING YOUR FEARS

When I dare to be powerful—to use my strength in the service of my vision, then it becomes less and less important whether I am afraid.

—Audre Lorde

Thousands of people of all ages and backgrounds share a fear of flying. Their minds are filled with terrifying images. They picture that moment when they know it's about to happen, like those final forty-five seconds before Flight 1549 hit the water. Some refuse to ever get on an airplane. Some fly reluctantly while calling upon all kinds of aids, healthy or otherwise, to get them through the flight. Those people would understand, as we all do, if the Hudson River landing triggered an old or new fear of flying for the passengers sitting in that cabin. That's what's happened to Don. He never really loved flying as some do, but it didn't really scare him, either. His fear sure wasn't holding him back when the plane went down, and he was sitting next to a side exit door. "I was just thinking, I've got to get off this plane. Got to see my wife and my son," he recalls. "And then I just went to open that emergency exit door as fast as

*I could." But now, just the thought of being in a plane again
terrifies him.*

*Don discussed this fear openly with me through our visit
that took us from a hotel lobby to his workplace to a friend's
home for pizza. A highly responsible parent, husband,
employee, and friend, he is at ease revealing all the details
of this fear and how he's reacted to suddenly having it.
Others might not want to go there. It takes courage to admit
to your vulnerability, in all its awkward and potentially
embarrassing colors. It's easy to hide it, easier still to deny
it. But Don has that courage. He respects his fear and he
lets others know it's there. And as you will see in his story,
that vulnerability is serving him, and those around him, in
new and profound ways.*

—Kevin

In Don's Words

I REMEMBER THE FIRST TIME I ever felt afraid from an airplane
experience. I was en route from Connecticut to Tuscon, Arizona,
to begin living with my grandmother because my parents had
divorced and my mother was not healthy enough to care for me.
I was traveling alone . . . and I was five years old.

The flight itself actually didn't bother me. I had my picture books and crayons to keep me busy, and I liked flying
like a bird. A flight attendant watched me like a hawk and
kept me supplied with snacks and drinks. The landing was

easy enough, but when I hopped down the steps and tiptoed out onto the tarmac, I could not see my grandmother anywhere. I was abandoned!

"Donny! Donny! Over here!" a voice finally called out. After the flight attendant made sure this really was my grandmother, I ran up and hugged her until all the fear poured out of my skin.

I don't remember being asked to fly alone as a child again. My uncle Frank did his best to get me to love the world of airplanes and flying. He would keep me out of school for a day and drive me to JFK Airport where we would sit for hours just watching all the planes take off. We even witnessed an early takeoff of the Concorde to London or Paris. I didn't share Uncle Frank's enthusiasm, but I stuck with the plane-watching routine for him.

When he took me to Los Angeles for vacation, I remember the rides at Disneyland and sneaking onto the Paramount movie lot better than any view out the airplane window. Uncle Frank went on to a career in the airline industry; I went on to maintain a mostly amicable though far from passionate relationship with flying.

Then along came Flight 1549. When Sully said, "Brace for impact," and I realized I was sitting on the exit row, I studied those directions. When we crashed I went right to work and got that door opened and out of the way fast. You had better believe I am proud in knowing that I helped ensure the rapid exit of many other passengers. We all did what we could, what we needed to do. That's why we're all alive.

When my boss Darren contacted our CEO, and he arranged for a private plane to fly us out of Teterboro, New Jersey, that night, I was all for it. It helped that I was with Darren as well as my coworker Ben, and Molly, the wife of another coworker. The four of us and a fifth passenger were whisked out of the ferry terminal by police and rushed to the airport.

At Teterboro we were greeted by a hearty assortment of food and adult beverages our CEO had arranged for us. As I walked across the tarmac, holding a bottle of wine in each hand, wearing only the socks and sweatshirt provided by the Red Cross along with my soggy pants, I felt giddy. It didn't matter a bit that I was not wearing shoes. I strode confidently up to the large private jet that I assumed would take us to Charlotte. "No, we're over here," an airport official said, pointing to the six-seat plane we would fly. A month later I never would have gone near such a thing. But on this night, riding the high of surviving that crash, it didn't faze me. When winds met our celebrating party as we approached Charlotte, rocking our little plane from side to side, I muttered, "Please, just let us land safely," and we did. Flying was still okay.

But that night, after my joyful reunion with my wife Elizabeth and two-and-a-half-year-old son, Ethan, I stayed up all night studying every news story and every photo of the Flight 1549 crash landing on the Hudson. I was seeking answers: *How did this happen? What determines success and failure when a plane goes down? Had there been other bird strikes that knocked out plane engines and caused a crash?* I had just become a devoted student of the whys and where-

READER/CUSTOMER CARE SURVEY

HEFG

We care about your opinions! Please take a moment to fill out our online Reader Survey at **http://survey.hcibooks.com.**
As a **"THANK YOU"** you will receive a **VALUABLE INSTANT COUPON** towards future book purchases
as well as a **SPECIAL GIFT** available only online! Or, you may mail this card back to us.

(PLEASE PRINT IN ALL CAPS)

| First Name | | MI. | Last Name |

| Address | | | City |

| State | Zip | Email |

1. Gender
- ☐ Female   ☐ Male

2. Age
- ☐ 8 or younger
- ☐ 9-12   ☐ 13-16
- ☐ 17-20   ☐ 21-30
- ☐ 31+

3. Did you receive this book as a gift?
- ☐ Yes   ☐ No

4. Annual Household Income
- ☐ under $25,000
- ☐ $25,000 - $34,999
- ☐ $35,000 - $49,999
- ☐ $50,000 - $74,999
- ☐ over $75,000

5. What are the ages of the children living in your house?
- ☐ 0 - 14   ☐ 15+

6. Marital Status
- ☐ Single
- ☐ Married
- ☐ Divorced
- ☐ Widowed

7. How did you find out about the book?
(please choose one)
- ☐ Recommendation
- ☐ Store Display
- ☐ Online
- ☐ Catalog/Mailing
- ☐ Interview/Review

8. Where do you usually buy books?
(please choose one)
- ☐ Bookstore
- ☐ Online
- ☐ Book Club/Mail Order
- ☐ Price Club (Sam's Club, Costco's, etc.)
- ☐ Retail Store (Target, Wal-Mart, etc.)

9. What subject do you enjoy reading about the most?
(please choose one)
- ☐ Parenting/Family
- ☐ Relationships
- ☐ Recovery/Addictions
- ☐ Health/Nutrition
- ☐ Christianity
- ☐ Spirituality/Inspiration
- ☐ Business Self-help
- ☐ Women's Issues
- ☐ Sports

10. What attracts you most to a book?
(please choose one)
- ☐ Title
- ☐ Cover Design
- ☐ Author
- ☐ Content

TAPE IN MIDDLE; DO NOT STAPLE

BUSINESS REPLY MAIL

FIRST-CLASS MAIL PERMIT NO 45 DEERFIELD BEACH, FL

POSTAGE WILL BE PAID BY ADDRESSEE

Health Communications, Inc.
3201 SW 15th Street
Deerfield Beach FL 33442-9875

FOLD HERE

Comments

fores of air travel—not the joy, excitement, and allure that propelled my uncle Frank into his steadfast love but the harsh, frightening, often deadly side that haunts so many people all over our country.

Still, I didn't hesitate when Darren, Ben, and I got the call a few days later to fly to LA to appear on *The Ellen DeGeneres Show*. I didn't even object when a rare snowfall greeted the Charlotte area the day we were to leave. The flights were okay, the show was a blast, and while I kept reading all about air crashes and aircraft safety records, all this new and alarming knowledge wasn't holding me back.

Weeks later I was in a plane again, this time for a surprise birthday party for my brother Shane in Connecticut. We've always been close, and I had not seen him since the crash. So when his girlfriend, Stacey, told me her plan, I made a posting on Facebook that said: "Watch out, geese, here I come!" I even booked a flight to LaGuardia, which didn't bother me until the plane approached New York, and the pilot abruptly halted his approach, within site of the runway, and thrust upward. "Sorry," he announced, "we've lost separation with another aircraft." In other words, we got too close to another airplane and could have collided!

Still, I managed to keep images of the Hudson at bay, and soon I was rejoicing in my reunion with Shane. But back at home, I had moved into plane crash graduate studies. I got sucked in by the website airsafe.com, with links like "Fatal Events" by Airline, Recent Crashes, and Aircraft Model. Pretty dramatic stuff. My head was swimming with facts and figures

about plane crashes and near-crashes all over the world. I
was jolted by the reminder of the 1989 US Air LaGuardia-to-
Charlotte flight that crashed into the East River. That plane,
unlike ours, did break up when it struck the water, and
though sixty-one people survived, two did not.

Then that string of new "events" were soon added to airplane history: Colgan Air Flight 3407, a Q400 turboprop,
that crashed near Buffalo, killing all fifty on board in
February. The FedEx cargo plane, an MD-11, that crashed in
Japan, killing both crew members in March. The Pilatus PC-
12 that crashed in Montana, killing all fourteen passengers,
including seven children. The Air France, spotless-record
Airbus A330 that crashed in the Atlantic Ocean, killing all
228 on board. The Yemenia Airbus 310 crash in which only
one girl from France survived.

Each fatal crash hit me hard, as it did most of my fellow
survivors. Each person on each of those flights left a whole
world behind them, just as it could have been for our
families. The Buffalo crash was the big blow. The first. I was
up before 5 a.m. the morning after the crash, as I often am,
reading the news on the Internet. As soon as I saw the headline, I flipped on CNN. "That could have been us!" I said to
myself. "If Sully had tried to go to Teterboro, we probably
would have crashed into a residential area in New Jersey. And
that's what would have happened." Each time I would see the
photo of another passenger from the Buffalo crash, my heart
sank lower.

In April, when I was assigned to fly to Los Angeles to complete a deposition for work, I became a bit jittery during the flights out from Charlotte to Phoenix and Phoenix to Orange County. I can't say I was specifically thinking about those recent plane crashes. I just knew that I didn't want to be on a plane anymore. When it was time to go home, via the red-eye out of Orange County, I was anxious hours before I got to the airport. As we taxied out on the runway, I remembered how when a flight takes off from Orange County Airport, noise ordinances require pilots to head almost straight up and then shut the engines off briefly. Or so it seems. Those few seconds of quiet brought back the silence before Sully's command: *Brace for impact.* Flying was not okay now! At each little bit of turbulence, I was jumping in my seat.

When I got off that plane in Phoenix, I thought that was it. I was going to take a bus, a train, or a one-way car rental all the way back to North Carolina. But I gritted my teeth and said, "I can do this. I *need* to do this for work. I can get through it." Before the boarding call, I was itching all over, literally breaking out in hives. "I can do this. I *need* to do this. . . ." I made it home, itching all the way, but then I vowed to do whatever it took to stay out of airplanes. With Darren's support, I found ways to complete work deals via phone or to substitute coworkers for necessary air travel. I visited a post-traumatic stress counselor who assured me that my feelings were normal.

Still, though you might think it strange, I kept scouring all the news about plane crashes. I even watched the spring '09 episode of *Lost* on ABC when they showed another crash that sent many characters back to the island, as well as those images of the crash that launched the series. Another night I stumbled upon *Final Destination* on a movie channel. I happened to come in just when the male character sitting on a plane with fellow high school students has a premonition that their plane is going to crash. In his image, people are sucked out of the plane and fire burns his face, before he wakes up. He convinces some of his friends to join him in getting off the plane, but others choose to stay on. And the plane crashes, just as he imagined it!

Why do I watch? I rationalize that I can separate fiction from reality. Sometimes I wonder if it's actually some sort of therapy for my anxiety about flying. Maybe in the watching of it all, I can slowly begin to let go of how it torments me. Time will tell.

Gratefully, my fear of flying has not been the only by-product of surviving the crash on the Hudson. Far from it. First, it has left me much less prone to bouts of anger and impatience at home, at work, everywhere. I'm more tolerant of people and frustrating situations. Also, I used to lose hours of sleep worrying about work deadlines and demands. Now I don't lose a minute.

More important, it has made me a better dad—a *much* better dad, hopefully. Before, when Ethan would act like a brat, as kids sometimes do, I would get frustrated and walk away. If he threw something, I'd get angry. Now I just hold him. If he needs to scream, he can scream in my arms. And while I hug him, I just think how I could have missed this, *all* of this:

watching *Toy Story* for the tenth time with his head on my lap; chasing him around while he playfully shouts, "Get Ethan, get Ethan"; or sighing when he says, "Daddy, plane broken." Before the crash when he would come up to me while I was working at home I would say, "Not now, Ethan, Daddy's busy." Now I stop and engage with him.

I shudder when I think of him almost having to live from the age of two without a father. That was my life; I would never ever want to repeat that for him. My most vivid memory of having a father is the huge scar on my leg from the time he hoisted me up on his Harley and my leg got embedded between the tire and rim. I was three. Now my son is three, and I get to create a different record book. How could anything fill me with more gratitude?

Also, I've cultivated a stronger spiritual connection. I've always struggled with organized religion. I grew up Catholic and converted to Judaism for my wife, but I've never been a regular churchgoer. I do believe there is a God and a reason for everything, though. I don't know that being closer to God is my calling. Maybe it's just helping people more. I'm always willing to talk to the media about our crash, so people can see that no matter what their challenges or struggles may be, it really doesn't have to be so bad, so hopeless. They can still get up every day and appreciate the sunshine, and the rain. They can still breathe. They can still love.

People used to tell me I was a good listener. I listen more now. Maybe, with my new fear of flying, I'm more understanding and compassionate. I can appreciate what's hard for

you, because this is hard for me. And maybe it all won't seem
so hard as we go forward, together.

Survival Brothers

*We're like a family. That's what so many passengers of
Flight 1549 say in describing the vital bonds that have
emerged from sharing the day that most of them thought
would be their last on earth. Of course, some passengers,
like Diane Higgins and Lucille Palmer, already were family.
They had that blood tie to lean on throughout the trauma
and every step of the aftermath. Others were total strangers.
Some fell somewhere in between: coworkers who knew each
other but did not relate with the closeness of family, until
they survived a plane crash together. That's how it's been
for Darren Beck and Don Norton, who work in the same
department at LendingTree in Charlotte.*

*"I knew Darren before. He's actually my supervisor,"
explains Don. "But after the crash we became closer very
quickly. We understood the ups and downs we were both
going through. When I had trouble during those first few
weeks keeping my focus at work, I knew he would understand. He'd tell me he was having the same problem. We
cared about each other."*

*Darren recalls the moment his friendship with Don really
took hold: on that flight back to Charlotte from Teterboro,
New Jersey, on a small chartered plane only hours after the
crash.*

"We just talked the whole way back," Darren explains.

"And the bond has gotten stronger at work. We don't keep a stuffy environment at LendingTree anyway, and I can kid Don about doing a new media interview about the crash every five minutes. I call him 'Prime Time' now."

"And I kid Darren about doing an interview two hours after the crash where he was making jokes about the Airplane movies with Peter Graves," counters Don. "The connection we have feels like having another brother."

"When Don and his family came over to our home for lunch one Saturday, and his son Ethan slipped and fell into our swimming pool, I dove in and scooped him up like he was one of my own sons," adds Darren, the father of three boys.

When Ellen DeGeneres offered a December cruise to all eight Flight 1549 survivors who appeared on her show soon after the crash, Darren and Don immediately committed to going together with their entire families. They both believe their new personal bond also strengthens their sense of teamwork on the job. When they go out for a work lunch together, they notice the difference.

"Instead of just talking about work as we would have before, we talk about . . . things I usually don't talk about with anyone else!" admits Darren. "We have complete trust in one another."

15
Debbie Ramsey:
SLOWING DOWN

*Slow down and enjoy life. It's not only the scenery
you miss by going too fast—you also miss the sense
of where you are going and why.*

—Eddie Cantor

As I talk to Debbie Ramsey on the phone, she is sitting on
her porch, speaking with her warm Southern accent. I picture her wrapped in a Red Cross blanket, a picture I've seen,
a moment she's talked about. I hear a plane go overhead—
on her end. She hears it too and says, "Wait a minute, I'm
going inside." I wonder, after the fact, whether she went
inside because of the noise or because of the memories.

Debbie's story is not quite the happily-ever-after story.
She is suffering from post-traumatic stress and is thankfully getting the help for it that she needs. But the night-
mares are frequent, the lack of sleep is unsettling, and on
top of that, for reasons that aren't really clear, she lost her
job. She could be the person cursing her fate, thinking this
awful experience ruined her life. But she's not. She's experiencing what everyone does at some key times in life, the
difficulties that life throws at us. We can easily get caught

in feeling victimized. We may spend much of our lives judging things as good or bad. And then we are either happy or mad. But truthfully, human beings and the lives we live are more complicated than that. For Debbie this is both a difficult, painful time and a wonderful, life-affirming time. She is both scared and excited. Debbie is learning the lessons that she knows she needs to learn. This is, after all, the only thing we can take from a difficult situation: a learning that moves us to a better life.

And what we know is that Debbie is held, at a deeper level than either her ups or downs, by family and by faith. Debbie's faith is clear and it held her as the plane was going down, during the rescue, and in all these months following. And like her faith, her family and her love of family has been sustaining. She's always loved her family, but now she loves them with more awareness of how very dear they are to her. They hold her that way too.

All of us have good days and bad days. Debbie's are just, at this time, a little more dramatic, as she revisits the trauma and as she leaves it behind, sometimes, to live fully in the present. Change includes difficulty. Faith includes suffering. As Debbie moves forward toward her own healing, she is blossoming. Both the trauma and the renewed faith are creating a stronger, more resilient person. And Debbie stops, now, to smell the roses, something she had forgotten about for many years.

—Dorothy

In Debbie's Words

I'M JUST A COUNTRY GIRL. I went from being the Kentucky-born youngest child of eight, with a coal miner dad and a homemaker mom, to a New York–commuting fashion expert and business manager, living in the fast lane. I was born and raised a Baptist, but hadn't been practicing much for years. Now I go to church every day. But none of this has been easy.

Our stuff came today—all my clothes and everything in the suitcase. They got it out of the wreck and sent it to California, I guess to see if there was anything else that caused the crash. It came back all cleaned and in plastic, and it was really hard for me. I've had a bad time of it, and at the same time I thank God every day to be alive. But I have night-mares, and I can't sleep, and I'm anxious a lot. Right after the accident, I was going to speak at a cancer survivor's group, but I was too anxious. I'm ready now, though. But I'm going to speak at my church. That seems safer.

I loved my busy life. It was so different from what I had grown up with. I loved working all the time, being busy, making money, being ahead of the game. I started traveling with my job, going to New York on what we call Fashion Street to buy new trends for the stores. I loved doing this. I loved New York. It was something I always wanted to do.

I put my family on hold for this company. I didn't know it then, but I do now: I was letting life pass me by. The week before the trip (my last business trip), I heard an inner voice telling me not to go. I also knew, somewhere that I didn't quite listen to, that my life wasn't what I wanted it to be any-more. I didn't like my job as much as I pretended I did. I was beginning not even to like myself. I knew I was missing something and secretly I knew what it was. I was missing my grandson Jack, I was missing my family, I was missing the quality of my life, and I was missing God.

"Jerry, I don't think I should go on this trip," I said to my husband.

"Of course you should, honey," he answered. "You love New York."

I said this a few times, to my son, to my boss, but no one, including me, believed that I should stay. After all, I loved this stuff. I loved the busy life. I loved being ahead of the game. And truth be told, New York was still fun—busy, busy, busy, going from here to there, never stopping, rushing like everybody else, just like New Yorkers!

As I was leaving for this flight north, I turned and looked for an especially long time at my husband. "I love you." In a spat with this man I love, I have been known to say, I'm sorry to admit, "You're gonna miss me when I'm gone!" I'm so very glad I hadn't said that to him in a while. I know I will never say it again.

Coming home is always the best. I've always been a bit ner-vous about planes, but coming home seems easier—the trip is over . . . almost. We were late. I've taken lots of flights between Charlotte and New York, but this was the biggest plane I'd ever been on. That didn't make me happy, and I was seated in 13A. I called my husband from the plane. "Honey,

I'm going to miss my plane in Charlotte." Little did we know how very much I was going to miss my plane. "Engines are revving up. Gotta go. Love you."

How somebody can relax on a plane is beyond me, but my seatmate looked like he was already asleep before we started moving. I didn't expect to have much conversation on this flight. I did get an "Oops!" from him when his cell phone rang while we were taxiing. When the *boom* came, and I saw fire coming from the engine, I got his attention (I'm thinking he was already wide awake himself). "What happened?" I asked.

"We lost an engine."

"Can we fly with just one?"

"Yep," he told me reassuringly. "We'll just head back to the airport." I started to call my husband again, but stopped myself. *Why worry him? No sense both of us being scared. I'll do it when we land.*

I could smell smoke. I heard a voice somewhere nearby: "The plane is on fire!"

I was really scared. My seatmate pointed out the window. "Look, it's Yankee Stadium—the old one and the new one."

I could see the stadiums and the many other buildings that were now higher than we were . . . and the river. *This is not good*, I thought. Of course, I was right.

The man I thought would sleep during this trip told me to hold on to the back of my seat. "Hold on as tight as you can. It's going to get rough!" Somehow, though, before I grabbed that seat, I opened my cell phone to look at the picture of

Jack, my three-year-old grandson. All I could think of was my family. I heard other people praying out loud. I heard a baby crying. I was preparing myself to die. I was missing Jack. And I was praying, like everybody else, I'm sure. And I was suddenly at peace. I was really at peace. I wasn't afraid. I felt God right before the impact. I knew whether I died or not, that it would be okay. It was so amazing to have such a peaceful feeling in a very scary and helpless situation. But I did, and my life was changed forever.

When the plane hit, then stopped, I got up from my seat, and then I turned around and looked back to see if I was still sitting in it! I couldn't believe I was still alive, and I guess I was just checking it out. Since I wasn't in the seat, I was alive, and I knew that I would stay alive. And I was scared, almost to the point of panic, back and forth with myself. "Please somebody, let me out. Please just calm down." I don't even know if I was talking out loud or just thinking. I grabbed my seat cushion, though. Even scared, I was thinking. And though it occurred to me to take my purse, which had chocolates in it for Jack, and I had a momentary consideration of taking my down jacket, I was thinking clearly enough to know not to do that.

Then it got hard. We were in freezing water, and I got out onto the wing, but slipped off. I started to panic again and was trying unsuccessfully to calm myself. "Calm down. I'll help you," I heard, when a hand reached down and pulled me up. I felt it as the hand of God. I don't know who he was. I wouldn't recognize him. But feeling, again, the presence of

God, through this man, I became calm. We inched back slowly on the wing and waited. Amazingly, on the wing, clinging to a stranger, surrounded by many others, wet through and through, I got out my cell phone once more. It shouldn't have worked. It was as wet as I was. The picture of Jack was right there when I opened it, and I got through to my husband. Another gift, another reminder of what was really important to me, another moment of grace.

Later when we were climbing up the netting to be rescued, my feet were caught, and they were so cold. I was pulling myself hand over hand and someone below me, trying to get up, grabbed my pants and I started to slip. But there was help . . . again . . . a hand on my bottom, pushed me right up. I don't know who that was, either. But it, too, felt like the hand of God. Thank you, whoever you were. That push gave me a surge of strength, and I got up the netting and into the boat. Then it was my turn to be the helper. People were cold. "We have to stay warm," I told one man, and we started to rub each other. A girl who was soaked started to sit alone and away from other folks, but I pulled her into our huddle, and we started rubbing her.

There were so many helpers, so many rescuers, so many places where people were touched and helped. So much goodness. The hand of God everywhere guiding us.

I knew I'd carry that generous spirit with me past this accident. For years I haven't been very close to my mother and sister and brothers—time, work, distance, all the things that can take over. I don't quite know what happened with my family. But now I'm closer to all of them. My mom is eighty-four and doesn't understand the seriousness of this accident, but she feels the changing relationship with me. It's a good thing. And right after the accident, a local family lost their house in a fire. The usual response from me would be to feel a moment of sorrow for these folks and get on with my life. This time, I gathered clothes and took them to the family. I also did another simple thing that is changing my life. I shared my story in a testimonial at my church, even though I was afraid of speaking. I didn't set out to be a helper, just to live my newfound truth, but one man (a stranger) called to say, "Thank you. You helped save my marriage." I feel I am sharing the touch of God that saved me, in little ways day-to-day.

There's so much to be thankful for. I get up every morning and feel thankful. But I was so shaken after the accident that my doctor told me to take time off from work, and when I went back a month later, I was under doctor's orders to work only part-time. I got fired! I don't understand that. It doesn't seem fair. I've worked for them for close to nine years. And still I'm carrying this whole thing in a way that's not so good for me, not sleeping, anxiety, nightmares . . . and then this.

But I'm getting help. I'm working with someone and writing. Writing helps. And mostly what I'm doing that I just forgot to do in the last years of my life is slowing down. I have a family that loves me, but I got busy, busy, busy. Just doing everything. Now I slow down. Now I always take the time to smile at people and say, "How are you?" It's a better life. In spite of the hard stuff, I wouldn't change this experience. Now I am living my life. I've been touched, I've been hurt,

I've been scared, and I'm really here now. I have things to say and I'm getting ready.

For the first time, I'm taking a look at my life and seeing what is important for me, not just what pleases others. I was letting life pass me by and now I know God has a purpose for me. For the last ten years I've put God on the back burner. I had him in my heart but I just wouldn't and didn't have time. Now I know how to stop and listen—to others and to my own instincts. I care. I have so much power that wants to help. I want to be able to make a difference in this world.

What's changed for me? I'm letting myself cook, which I love to do but rarely had time. I'm spending more time with my husband. We've been married twenty-three years, but we both got on the fast track and hardly noticed. I'm thinking about a new career, but I'm not in a rush and that's already amazing. I had always wanted to be in the fashion industry. The coal miner's daughter did just that, and I know I've done enough of that now. I've got something in my heart that I didn't have before, and I'll give it some time to see where it takes me, but I'm sure my new career will be about helping. I've been helped so much. I don't see how I could not return that.

When my grandson was born three years ago, I knew I had been given a gift, but it took this accident for me to pay attention to that gift. That's what has changed most. I took him to the zoo yesterday, and I had nothing else I needed to do. I am not busy. I am here for my life, for those I love and for others in need. This is what I have truly been given. I am blessed.

16
Billy Campbell:
COMING HOME

> Home is not where you live, but where they
> understand you.

> —Christian Morganstern

Billy Campbell lives a Los Angeles lifestyle. He's one of the few passengers from the West Coast . . . though it's not where he hails from. If you were to see him in LA, you might see him in the company of famous people, as he knows many of them. He's been in the TV industry for years, and once was president of Discovery Networks. And he has loved that life. He's still doing business in LA these days. But Billy grew up in Greenville, South Carolina, in a house-hold in which the rule was no TV-watching except for one night a week. Usually that meant catching an ACC college basketball game with his mom on a Wednesday night or perhaps an episode of Hill Street Blues with his dad. His career has shocked many childhood friends.

But that's only a part of who he is. Billy is a deep believer in God, in helping others, in family. He was, in fact, on his way to his home in Litchfield Beach, South Carolina, close to his family, when the accident happened. Instead of the *short trip he had planned, he ended up staying quite a while. As I listen to him recount that time and what came after it, I sense that his stay back in South Carolina was more than a recuperation break. I wonder if Billy was also reclaiming his roots, sifting through his past to see how to reapply it to who he is and what he's doing now with this second chance at life. Coming home, at this particular time, has opened the door to a fresh perspective for him. That's a potentially fruitful step for any of us in the midst of upheaval, or just a period of reevaluating our goals, priorities, and life direction. And after taking that step, we watch to see what may emerge. Billy is watching . . . and acting on what he sees.*

—Kevin

In Billy's Words

WHEN THE MIRACLE HAPPENED, I had been in an interim period of my career. After years with TV networks, I had tried a couple of different ventures—looking for something new that would excite me. But when I flew back to South Carolina the day after the crash, I decided to put all that looking on hold for awhile.

I had family waiting to see me. Mom had driven over to meet me, just as she was going to pick me up from Myrtle Beach on the day of the crash. I called her from the life raft that day, hoping she wouldn't have to hear about it first on the radio. My sister Kara was there with her two boys, my nephews: Campbell, eight, and Billy, six. I kid her that she's got to call the older one first or she'll always be going around yelling "Billy Campbell!" The boys came up to me, gave me one big hug, and said, "Uncle B, we're so glad you're alive. Now can we throw the pigskin?" That was a sweet moment, a reminder of the resiliency of life and youth. I'm still a big kid at heart, and I loved being with them then.

So I stayed around. The original plan was to spend a long weekend to rest up, catch up, and maybe do a little duck hunting. But I soon let those plans go. I look back on those three or four weeks now as the process of peeling back an onion. I was going through layers of thinking through what happened from the crash on the physical front, the mental and psychological front, and the spiritual front.

With the physical side, when I left New York I had a bump on my head from getting knocked into the seat in front of me when we hit the water. I felt okay, but while I was back home I met two former college roommates who are now surgeons. "You need to understand something here, Billy," one friend said. "The adrenaline was pumping, and that can carry you for twenty-four to thirty-six hours. But then it wears off. You need to take care of yourself."

Sure enough, after thirty-six hours I had a familiar feeling. I had been a high school football player and suddenly I felt as sore and banged up as I would from three-a-day practices wearing pads. My triceps were almost burning. "Well, that makes sense," I said to myself. "I had to climb over all those seats to get out, and that was a lot of hoisting." So I took care of myself.

The psychological side would come in when I was around other people. They all wanted to know about the crash. A near-death experience like this is one of those seminal events. How did you survive against all odds? It could have happened to anyone, and since it happened to me, people wanted to know how I felt. They would marvel at being around me. "I know you're probably sick of talking about it," many would begin, but I'd quickly reassure them, "I understand. You're asking because you care. If I were you, I would ask, too." I would even help them when I saw them struggling to get out the question they most wanted to know: *Did I think I was going to die?* My answer: *You bet.*

So I relive my feelings about it all. I consider how I've always been a relatively reserved person. And I've always wanted to be in control. It was such a unique feeling on that plane to be suddenly so out of control. I had a window seat, and as we got closer to landing I looked out at the Hudson and said to myself, "You've got to be kidding." We were going to crash in the Hudson, and there was nothing I could do about it.

Looking at the mental part during that time at home moved me quickly to the spiritual side, as it always does. God wasn't ready to take me that day. He has another plan, something else in mind for me. I don't know what it is yet. Maybe that's why I decided to seek out the normalcy of being around home for a while. After that period at home, I went back to LA and jump-started several new ventures. I'm producing a Broadway musical, *Robin and the 7 Hoods,* due to launch at the Old Globe Theatre in San Diego in summer 2010. I'm still sorting out many other prospects, but I don't worry about where they all might take me or what else will emerge. I know he will lead me.

I've always been calm about what comes next, how things will work out. You can only do your best. I remember a high school basketball game when our team was down one point and I was going to the line to shoot a one-and-one free throw with one second left. That means if I missed that first shot, there would be no second shot. We would lose. If I made both shots, we would win. I wound up making them both, and we won. People asked me later if I was nervous. "No," I replied, "that's the reason you play the game." But you know something? I could have missed that first free throw, and it would have been okay because I would have lost while trying my best. It's not something to be nervous about. To me, getting nervous is never a positive thing. When you're nervous, it's harder to think and use your abilities. I believe that most pressure is self-induced. I've always believed that but now I find it extraordinarily true.

Something else was changing on my spiritual side. Like many folks on the plane, I was invited to speak at churches. My first talk was delivered to a Confirmation class at a church in North Carolina. I told them about remembering when I had been studying for my own Confirmation. "It seems like yesterday, but it's been thirty-six years," I said. "Those thirty-six years have gone by much too quickly."

I spoke about miracles, of course. Our miracle. This led me to discussing the importance of faith. Here are parts of what I shared:

We all have many disappointments in life. People hurt our feelings. We want a certain grade in class. We want to make a certain team. Sometimes we lose jobs that we need or that we love, and sometimes we even lose people that we love, our family members or our friends. Over the past two years I've lost several good friends and even some of my relatives. It's hard, and I've been quite sad, but I know that God has a plan. Often I may not completely understand it, but I trust him. When a door closes, another opens, and amazingly it seems to be for the better.

The hardest part for me about faith is not knowing. I've always been impatient so I've always wanted to know: What's the answer? What's next? Where am I going? And guess what? I've learned that I'm not always going to get the answer. Things will happen that I don't fully understand and sometimes that I even disagree with or become angry about. But the comforting part has been to learn that God doesn't always make things crystal clear to me. He may have a few twists and turns in the road that I didn't fully understand nor see coming. I could spend the rest of my life wondering: Why was I on Flight 1549 that day, at that hour? Why were those geese flying at that altitude, at that second? But as I've learned to accept it all as his will, it's made all the difference in the world.

Was I going to die that day? It didn't look so good, but I felt that if God wanted me or needed me, I was ready. In the end, He clearly wasn't ready for me. I was comforted by, "Yea though I walk through the valley of the shadow of death, I will fear no evil" (Ps.#23:4). I said to the Lord, "If you've decided that this is my time, I'm ready." It was a moment of peaceful tranquility.

God may take me tomorrow. If I have a say, he'll give me another forty-nine years. But that's not my call. What is my call is to believe that he has a plan for me, wants me to cherish each and every day. Remember, every day is a miracle. Some days they're just bigger than normal. . . .

You are preparing for your Confirmation. I've just had mine. I think mine was a reconfirmation.

The talk went well. I enjoyed being around the kids. So when I got back to Los Angeles and an old roommate of mine asked me to speak to his son's elementary school class, I didn't hesitate. They asked great questions. One boy asked, "If your plane left later, do you think maybe there would have not been any geese?" I answered, "Maybe not those geese, but there might have been others." I enjoyed speaking to them, but what really touched me was what came after I went home. That teacher did a wonderful thing: all the kids sent me a thank-you note with something specific they remembered from what I shared, along with some kind of illustration. Those were amazing.

Later I was at a dinner party, and someone invited me to speak at a high school. I'm busy, but I said yes to that one, too. It's important to bring these messages from our miracle to kids. With the younger kids, I emphasize that you'll never know when you'll be called on to be a hero. Sully didn't know what he would be called on to do that day, but he was prepared. So I tell them to start planning now for that day when they may be asked to do something important.

"Do your best at school, and everything you do. Be as prepared as you can be," I say. "Maybe you won't have to guide a plane to a miracle landing, but someday you may see someone you know in your school, or even a stranger in the street, who needs your help. You can be ready to step up."

I've continued to give talks to schools, church groups, Rotary organizations. Going into the schools around LA has been especially gratifying. Being single, without children of my own, it's a great experience getting close to kids. I'm not sure what that may lead to for me, but as I said, I don't worry about it. Some of the new ventures I've been exploring recently have an educational component to them. I'm drawn to those because it's more important to me now that what I do in work will broaden and enrich my life as well as those I touch. That's my guiding compass.

So I'm back in my LA life, though I won't go long until heading back to South Carolina again. But you know, people really aren't that different anywhere you go. Recently I went to a movie in Century City with an agent and his friend. "You know, Billy was on that flight in the Hudson," the agent said.

"Oh, God!" the friend said. "I know you must be sick of talking about it, but I'd really like to hear about it."

The curiosity, the wanting to know, the wondering about being fifty-five seconds from death—it's universal. Like I said,

I would want to know, too. I lived it all and I'm still peeling back those layers of the onion.

P.S. In another connection to his South Carolina roots, Billy happened to bump into an old friend from Greenville while at the ferry terminal after the crash. It was fellow passenger Mark Hood, whose wife, Lisa, attended high school with Billy. Mark and Billy soon discovered that they were even on the same life raft without realizing it! This reunion was a special moment for both.

—Kevin

17
Ray Basri, M.D.:
HEALING AND HEALED

I'm a great believer in luck, and I find the harder I work the more I have of it.

—Thomas Jefferson

Ray Basri was a physician on scene on the New York side of the rescue effort. He was there, as he so often is, through a combination of hard work and luck. Ray is a physician and a long-time firefighter. Not your usual combination. But Ray is not your usual doctor. Ray's life has been about being there for other people, whether it is coaching his kids' teams, being a doctor in a small New York town, or being a volunteer firefighter. Thomas Jefferson's quote means a lot to Ray. Long before Flight 1549, Ray had seen and been involved in the darkest of tragedies, the saddest of situations, the most dangerous moments. As a firefighter he'd been in collapsing buildings, flashover fires, and other near-death situations. As a volunteer physician, he'd gone to Louisiana for Hurricane Katrina within the first few days, and he's been back many times, working with medical issues, teaching emergency preparedness, doing what he does best. Helping. "Practicing medicine is the most important thing in the world," he tells me.

Ray was also at the World Trade Center on the morning of the attacks and in the days that followed. He had rushed in because his sister worked across the street and he couldn't reach her. He stayed to help. "We were raised right, I know that. We appreciate what we have and we help others." Thankfully, his sister, Carole, also someone who gives freely of her time to those in need, was late to work that day.

Talking to Ray, I knew that more happened for him on January 15, 2009, than he realized in that moment. In a very real way, he was undoing some of the trauma of 9/11. All the triggers were there: sirens, unknown crises, NYC police and firefighters, and Ray, arriving on the scene to help. But this time, it was a miracle. For Ray it was not just the relief of this moment—it was the letting go of some old and deeply painful memories. When passenger Vicki Barnhardt decided to return to the scene of her rescue, in a story you will soon read, she was consciously choosing to confront scary memories. For Ray, it just happened, by the nature of his life's commitment.

—Dorothy

In Ray's Words

I'VE BEEN A PHYSICIAN in internal medicine and a volunteer firefighter for twenty-two years now. I didn't intend to become a firefighter. I always wanted to be a doctor, and that was my goal and the way I oriented my life, as both my father and brother were physicians. But when I took over my wife's uncle's medical practice in upstate New York, he invited me to a barbecue, and I went. "It's a fire department barbecue. Have you ever thought of being a firefighter?" he asked.

"Not since I was five!" I said. But I got hooked. I took all the training and loved it. Our ladder company was very aggressive. We really pushed when it came to fires. We'd go into dangerous situations for search and rescue. I had close calls a few times, but came out okay. Now that I'm older, I don't go into the burning buildings anymore. I'm a deputy county fire coordinator. I'm still involved. I'm still a firefighter.

My connection to these huge events—9/11, Katrina, and the miracle flight—all came about through unusual circumstances. Of course, it's not just coincidence. It's work. I am ready, prepared, and my intention is to be there when someone is in need. I happened to be in New York, on the East Side, on January 15. I was getting medical equipment. In my car, I heard the news: "Plane down in the Hudson. Commercial airliner!" *Holy Cow! That's right across town, a half-mile away!* I put my lights and sirens on, just as a New York fire chief's car went by, his lights and sirens blaring. I jumped in behind him, and we moved across town. Fast, but always doing what we're trained to do: paying attention to traffic, to pedestrians, to the lights, looking carefully at intersections. It was a chaotic scene, and dozens of police, firefighters, and ambulances raced to the river. While crossing Eleventh Avenue, a New York City Police

Emergency Services truck raced through the red light and slammed into me and kept going, not even slowing down after the collision. They nearly hit a crossing guard on traffic duty as well, but she managed to get out of the way. No one was hurt, thankfully, but the traffic lady was pretty shocked. We looked at each other for a second, and then we looked for the police truck, which was already a block away and turning toward the river. I thought, *This is okay. There is an airliner in the Hudson River, and we all need to get there.* My car wasn't in great shape after that, but it was drivable, and I figured it would all work itself out as it always does.

I kept going, though, and as I drove down the West Side Highway, I couldn't help but think about the last time I was racing down this road, heading to the Twin Towers. I oriented myself toward this new potential disaster. *Okay, what am I likely to find? Blunt trauma, deceleration injuries, near drowning, hypothermia?* I was readying myself. But when I got inside the West Side ferry terminal, I noticed it was calm and quiet. That was my first sign that things were not out of control. It was also my first sigh of relief. I reported to the EMS lieutenant in charge. "I'm a physician and a firefighter and I'm here to help." He said everyone was triaged green, except the flight attendant with leg injuries. She was yellow. Another sigh of relief. As the only doctor on the scene, I checked Doreen [the flight attendant] and gave the okay to transport her.

In New York, the rescue procedure is to send out MIRVs (Mass Incident Response Vehicles). They are staffed with docs and interns from local medical centers. Amazingly, they never had to come to this event. It was not a disaster. I wondered about the other passengers. Were any missing or still in the river? From the ferry passenger terminal, we could not see the river or any of the rescue activity. Several head counts later, it became clear that all were safe. There were no celebrations. It was quiet and subdued. It slowly began to dawn on me that this was a miracle.

Making the scene even more of an amazing event was the voice I heard calling, "Dr. Basri?" And there was Diane Higgins and her mother Lucille Palmer, friends and neighbors from our hometown of Goshen, New York. How could that be? Such a small world. I checked them out, making sure to take off Lucille's wet socks and shoes. It felt a little awkward to take out my camera, but we took a couple of photos because we could not believe the coincidence.

A few days later I stopped by their house and brought a bottle of champagne to celebrate. They are wonderful folks. I've known Diane's husband for many years from the local fire department where he is a commissioner, and he was, at that time, also running for mayor. I suggested that perhaps Diane should be the candidate, since she was clearly more famous and better looking!

It took me a while on the scene to soak in the reality that this was not a tragedy. People were talking quietly, some on cell phones, some sitting absorbed in their own thoughts. Coffee was being distributed to many cold, shaking hands, and people were getting warm clothes, settling in, being calm. There were many detectives, some FBI, and emergency management doing interviews of all the passengers. The flight

crew was a bit off to the side by the windows. They were smiling and confident. They said it was the only successful water
landing of a commercial airliner ever, and they had done it.
The captain, Chesley B. Sullenberger III, was standing farthest
away from the passengers, quietly accepting congratulations.
His uniform was as impeccably pressed as if he were boarding
his flight. He was soft-spoken and gracious.

Later I spoke with Mayor Bloomberg in the terminal.
Mayor Bloomberg is an accomplished fixed wing and rotary
pilot who had his own close call with a bird strike over the
Hudson River a couple of years earlier. He was flying his helicopter when a seagull hit the rotor, and he lost a lot of altitude in a couple of seconds. He did not declare an emergency,
and he did mange to fly his damaged copter back to
LaGuardia Airport. He spoke glowingly of the US Airways
pilot's and first officer's skill to bring the plane in safely, as
only one with firsthand experience can appreciate.

There really wasn't a lot for me to do as a physician. I spent
some time trying to meet some of the passengers. I asked if
there was anything I could do for them. One young man was
in his best suit and tie, and I went over and said to him, "You
look like you're going to an interview." He laughed and said
he had just done one before getting on the plane. Small world
again. . . . He's in medical school, as is his wife. He'd just done
an internship interview and it ended early, allowing him to be
on this flight rather than the later one he had planned on taking home. He said that he had another interview in Rhode
Island the following week and that he knew he had to fly

there. We laughed about not getting to make choices when you're a doctor. This was his first visit to New York City. I asked him not to judge the city by this one experience.

I always think that people need to use their abilities. That's why I'm well-trained and keep myself ready. It was a miracle that I was in the right place at the right time. But I don't think I could have taken another 9/11.

I finished up my stint at the rescue site by calling the Federal Aviation Authority. I reported all was well on the scene. My final sigh of relief.

What a different story this has been from the story of 9/11. That still haunts me. I got to Ground Zero a few minutes after the second tower collapsed. I went in with fire gear, to the base of the first tower. I managed to help a FDNY captain with a fractured arm coming out, but mostly there was no one to help. No search and rescue, just recovery. I was an older guy (forty-six at the time). Firefighters could relate to me, 'cause I was one of them. But there were kids on the scene—young guys, volunteers, in their teens and early twenties, just there to help and witness the devastation. I sent some of them away. No good would come of this for them. It was too awful and post-traumatic stress disorder (PTSD) would likely haunt them for years.

What I found out on January 15 was that maybe I was in need of a bit of healing myself. As I raced to the scene, I worried about facing another disaster, another scene of devastation and loss. It stirred up old feelings. But after my last sigh of relief, I had the thought, *God is always watching over me!*

Being a physician and a firefighter is my life's work.

Sometimes it is full of sadness and sometimes joy. I was pretty happy to walk away from that scene with the good feelings I had, knowing everyone was safe. The best thing, though, for me, after the crash landing, was a completion of the circle of my work, of the horror of 9/11 and the joy of January 15. Because some key people knew that I had been at 9/11 and saw me there at the Flight 1549 rescue, I was invited by the New York City Fire Department to join their World Trade Center monitoring program for the health of FDNY fire-fighters, current and retired, who were there on 9/11. I'm committed to being a firefighter working with medical issues, which is certainly not where I thought I'd be when I started my medical career and went to that first barbecue!

Now I'm working with everything from PTSD to some of the respiratory conditions caused by toxins and smoke. I am finally doing something positive about 9/11, and when I'm helping, I'm a much happier person. It is common for me to sit and listen to firefighters open up to discuss their pain and loss. Myself, I find it hard to open up to these same feelings, but I know I need to and I do. It helps me, and it helps me working with others who gave so much.

Finding a miracle when I expected a tragedy has been wonderful. Celebrating life and not facing death and loss has been a relief. Finding a way to keep helping those who have been so injured has been a further commitment in my life: one I have taken on gladly. Maybe there is a God up there! And besides, if you're a firefighter, being with the FDNY is like playing for the Yankees!

18
Vicki Barnhardt:
KNOWING WHEN TO GO BACK

Healing is a matter of time, but it is also sometimes a matter of opportunities.

—Hippocrates

The stories of how the passengers of Flight 1549 truly cared for one another on January 15 can inspire all of us to more faithfully look out for one another in times of crisis and need. Vicki Barnhardt benefited from one of the many acts of caring and selflessness after she jumped off one of the wings of the plane trying to reach a life raft, only to find herself unable to maneuver the frigid water. A male passenger swiftly and firmly reached his arms down into the cold and hoisted her back up, then guided her to a safer position. Vicki has thanked this unknown passenger hundreds of times in her mind and her heart.

She also recognized that for herself and her new community, the need for caring did not end after everyone had made it safely to the shores of the Hudson. That's why she launched the Facebook group "1549 Survivors." She hopes the caring that emerges from that forum will last over the long haul, and that the compassion and support from other *sources also lives on. "Sometimes the human tendency is to care in the moment but then sometimes it dissipates," she says. "Look at Hurricane Katrina. People are still suffering, but it's seen as old news. It's sad. I hope it's different for all of us."*

Vicki also understands that for anyone recovering from trauma, self-caring is critical. In the midst of emotional upheaval, we're in charge of discerning what will help and what will not. When we are vulnerable, we have choices about how we heal, and at what pace. Just before our phone interview, Vicki had faced one of those choices, this one regarding the important question of when and why to revisit the scene of her trauma. While ultimately that scene on the Hudson became a source of great relief and gratitude, it still was packed with raw emotions. Was it right to go back, or better to stay away? Vicki's choice, and what she experienced after making it, have much to offer us about caring, about being vulnerable, about healing.

—Kevin

In Vicki's Words

MY HUSBAND, MIKE, ERASED the phone message of the last words I thought I would ever speak to my family: "We've crashed. This is it. I just want to tell you I love you, I love the kids, I love you, I love you, I love you!" I was standing in waist-deep water in the aisle of the plane, firmly believing we had sunk. He didn't want to keep such a visceral reminder of that horrifying winter afternoon when he believed he had just become a widower and a single parent of our two children. I don't blame him. But you can't push a button to erase all the pain, the terror, and the deep, deep sadness behind the words. Those echoes live within me. I'm not sure if they will ever completely dissolve. Yet I am finding that with caring, time, and unexpected moments of lightness and warmth, they can at least begin to fade. . . .

In June 2009, five months after the crash of Flight 1549, I had scheduled a trip to New York to see a client in White Plains. "Let's go up early," Mike suggested. "We can stay in the city, make a weekend of it."

I knew what he was thinking. We had never actually explored New York City, so this would be an opportunity to see the sites: Broadway, Times Square, the Statue of Liberty, the major stores. But this was more than an invitation for a Southerner who grew up in Seneca, South Carolina, to at last see the real New York. Mike knew that I would also have the chance to go *there* again: the location of Flight 1549's crash landing on the Hudson River and our harrowing rescue.

Was I ready? Well, I certainly was not ready the only other time I had gone back to New York, for the interviews with a large contingent of passengers on the *CBS Early Show,* the day after Sully's appearance on *60 Minutes.* That was in early February, just a few weeks after the crash, in the midst of that New York winter that would always bring me right back to the stark memories of that cold, cold day. I was still emotionally numb, and there would not have been time to see much then anyway. We were flown into New York the evening before the show and roused about 3:30 a.m. for the predawn taping, then flown right back home. Anyway, I could not imagine walking down to the windy shore of the Hudson River. I just didn't need to be that close, that soon. But now it was June. The weather had warmed, five months had passed since the accident, and my emotions had . . . well, begun to settle down.

"All right," I said, "we'll make a weekend of it."

It felt somehow important to say yes to whatever this might be. I had been doing a great deal of reflecting on what happened, with my faith guiding me. This experience has cemented for me that none of us are in control of our lives; God is. On that day in January I feel certain he knew what was going to happen before it did, and what the outcome would be. He put that crew and passengers on that plane— it was part of his plan. I firmly believe there is a reason why all of us are still here. The reason may be very different for each person, and it may be something very simple. But while I continued to work through my own healing and the needs for my family, I was reminded *every day* of what a blessing it is to be here.

Not long before Mike's invitation, I had one of those moments when the grief over what almost was and the gratitude for what is got squeezed together. During one of those long family walks we cherish with our nine-year-old daughter, Samantha, and five-year-old son, Michael, I said to

myself, "I'm so glad to have this time with them! They're
growing up and I am here. . . ."

*On the phone, Vicki pauses to compose herself. Her soft
crying can be heard in the background.*

I lost my dad . . . on an airplane. He had a heart attack on a
flight from South Carolina to Texas. They detoured the plane and
made an emergency landing in Atlanta, but it was too late. He
probably died on that plane. I was fifteen. I didn't make the asso-
ciation before our plane went down, but while we were trying to
evacuate, one of my many thoughts was that I might actually get
to see him again . . . in heaven. It was a bittersweet yet peaceful
thought: I may not get to see my kids and husband again, but
after all these years I may finally get to see my dad. . . .

On the day of our June trip to New York, we left our home
outside Charlotte, drove to the airport, and checked in for our
flight to LaGuardia, the opposite direction of Flight 1549's
original route. I gladly took advantage of US Airways' offer of
an upgrade to first class for any of us who were on that flight.
It's not just for the extra legroom and more attentive service.
You need to understand that on that day in January, I had been
sitting in seat 26C, the very rear of the aircraft, the place that
absorbed the hardest hit and that frightening initial burst of
water that we feared could drown us. I will never sit anywhere
near the back of any airplane ever again.

Long before we reached LaGuardia, I began to wonder if I
should have stayed home. When you fly in June, one poten-

tial danger you don't face in January is a thunderstorm, and we got caught in a nasty one. In the past I would have laughed off any bouncy interlude or unexpected change of altitude. Not anymore.

"We've hit some heavy turbulence from the storm, and we will be making a detour to the southwest, where we hope the ride will be a bit smoother," the captain announced.

Detour? That's not a welcome airplane vocabulary word for me. *Let's just hope there are no more announcements.* When I looked outside and saw the stunning white flashes of lightning, my mind flashed to the Air France jet that might have been taken down by a thunderstorm. I leaned over to feel the warmth of my husband's shoulder and chest, and I softly cried.

But then the lightning disappeared, our plane returned to its normal route, and my tears dried. When we approached LaGuardia, I didn't flinch, wasn't thinking of the coincidence that the client I was heading to see in White Plains was the same client I had visited before boarding that flight bound for Charlotte on January 15. Perhaps time really does heal.

We checked into our room at Le Parker Meridien on Fifty-sixth Street, a great location to begin what I soon learned was the most repeated activity in New York City: walking. We trekked down Fifth Avenue, covered a long stretch of Broadway, perused Times Square, and stopped in FAO Schwarz long enough to consider what Samantha and Michael might like, which we quickly determined was practically everything. At the Carnegie Deli, Mike chomped into a BLT that they probably used an entire pig for, while we had a very New York experience: sitting with tables scrunched together and having to listen to two young men discuss details of their dating life. I was loving it all, but I also knew that I had another important mission: to see the dinner cruise ship with the name I couldn't recall, the scene of my most vivid memory of the Flight 1549 rescue.

I was on one of the wings, and at one point I thought I could swim to one of the life rafts. Only when I got in that thirty-something degree water, I could tell I was never going to make it. Thankfully, one of the male passengers somehow reached down and pulled me back up to the wing; I still don't know who it was. I shivered awhile longer. Then, while many passengers were picked up by one of the many NY Waterway commuter ferries that had swooped in toward our sinking plane, I was among those taken from the wing by one of the smaller, open-aired Coast Guard boats. We were packed in tight in the frigid conditions. As the wind pierced through my clothes and my skin, I was drenched to the bone—and probably still in shock. We heard that they had decided to bring us to a docked dinner cruise boat, probably because the triage center was not set up yet. We could warm up and await instructions on where to go next.

Stepping up the walkway and entering that dinner boat, I finally felt like I had really made it! I can still see fresh in my mind the image of walking onto that boat, my soaking life jacket from the plane still pressed tight against my cheek, as the New York firefighters and police officers wrapped us in the ship's white tablecloths until the Red Cross arrived with blankets and clothes. So warm, so safe. That moment cemented for me just how deeply we all had been cared for and how blessed we were from the moment we heard "Brace for impact."

Maybe it was that caring I had come to taste again now. I wanted to see that dinner cruise boat again. The trouble was, I didn't know exactly where it had been docked, and I hadn't done any research to help point the way. I was relying on my memory and the knowledge of New Yorkers to set me straight. Mike and I gave it a first run by walking the eight blocks from our hotel directly to the Hudson. Nothing looked familiar. When we approached a police officer and told him my story, he said, "Oh, you want to go to Chelsea Piers. That's more than thirty blocks down." I turned to Mike and said, "I think I'd like to take a cab."

So we returned to the hotel, and I changed from my tennis shoes to my flip-flops because I wasn't expecting to walk much. Bad move. When the cab dropped us off near Chelsea Piers, down around Twenty-third Street, nothing looked remotely familiar. We started approaching anyone who might know anything about the crash and rescue scene. The typical response: "Oh yeah, that was near the Intrepid. But the Intrepid wasn't there that day." So we walked and walked, lingering at one point to appreciate the beautiful landscaping on the shoreline near Thirty-fourth Street. Still no trace of that dinner cruise boat. As we kept walking back up toward midtown, we stumbled upon the NY Waterway pier.

"Come on, let's go on their tour boat," Mike said. "You can tell them who you are." I put up a hand. "Well, maybe we

can go on," I said, "but I don't know if I should say anything."
I always felt shy or hesitant about telling strangers about
being on Flight 1549. It was okay just to approach individuals near the river to ask for directions, but this would be different. Dozens of people would be on this boat.

Per our usual routine, Mike was the one who explained it to
the young woman at the ticket booth. "You were on that plane?"
she said. "Oh, no way! Listen, it's one p.m., and they're just
about to leave on the next tour. But I'll tell them to wait for you."

"That's very kind of you," I said. "But we haven't had lunch
yet. We didn't expect to be out so long."

"No problem!" she said, and then turned to a coworker
and added, "Fix them a sandwich. They can take it on the
boat with them."

I was touched by this act of caring. And as it turned out, our
tour guide had been on one of the ferries that had joined in the
rescue on January 15. "We've got to stop meeting like this,"
he quipped to me privately. When he told his usual story of
Flight 1549 to these tour passengers, he added an extra reference: "And ladies and gentlemen, we have one of the passengers of that flight on our boat with us here today!" Fortunately,
he didn't point me out. I wasn't ready to be *that* vulnerable.

As I glanced at all the warm, engaged faces, I understood
somehow that what happened on January 15 had been very
important to New Yorkers. They carry those other memories
of dramatic moments that did not end in exultation, so maybe
they were especially touched by what happened to us. Maybe
they shared in it. Even now, months after the miracle, they

cared—about the event, about us. Sitting on that ferry I was somehow feeling the caring of the city. We all care for one another as passengers, of course, and I am fortunate to field a steady stream of comforting responses on our Facebook group. But this New York caring was something . . . different.

Mike and I took dozens of pictures of the tour boat, of the Hudson, of the shoreline. He made sure to get a shot of me standing beside the many photos of our rescue that appeared on boats and busses. When we disembarked, we kept walking. Even in my flip-flops I was moving faster, lighter. We didn't have to go far. I saw tour busses lined up in a parking lot, just as I remembered them lined up that day, and then I spotted her.

"That's the dinner cruise boat!" I shouted. "The one closest to the water."

We were on Pier 81, where I understand the World Yacht tours operated from. We knew we weren't supposed to go down to the dock, but of course we did. I saw her name, the one I couldn't remember: *The Duchess.* "Come on, let's go in," said Mike, so gracious to share this moment with me on Father's Day. But I shook my head. "No, I'm good standing right here, thank you."

I smiled. I was more than good. On this beautiful seventy-degree late afternoon, darn close to the time of day when our plane went down near this very spot, I stood there in my khaki-colored capris, brown short-sleeved T-shirt, and my flip-flops, and just breathed it all in. "There's the ramp I struggled to walk up that day," I said to myself. "And there's the door . . . it's all just as I remember it."

19
Glenn Carlson:
EMBRACING COMMUNITY

I am of the opinion that my life belongs to the community, and as long as I live it is my privilege to do for it whatever I can.

—George Bernard Shaw

I know Glenn Carlson has much he could choose to talk about. Soon after the crash he reread Scott Peck's The Road Less Traveled *and found himself reconnecting with the concept of grace from the book. He also could talk a lot about his work or growing up in New Jersey. As a man who loves humor, he could offer a lively critique of current and former comedians. But from the start I recognize that what he really wants to focus on is a theme that I also want to explore: community. I have heard about the close community ties born from the Miracle on the Hudson, and I know that Glenn has been one of the main organizers in bringing passengers together.*

As he tells me what he's done and how it's served him and the other passengers, I remember an experience of my own. I had just moved to the San Francisco Bay area in 1989 when I rode the waves of the earthquake that knocked down the Bay Bridge. I was struck by how in the aftermath we all

*came together, guided by a simple phenomenon: crisis cre-
ates community. You see it among cancer patients or parents
who've lost children or almost any group that has shared
some life struggle or shake-up. Through the support and
camaraderie, spirits rise. Friendships form. It made sense
that after 150 passengers lived through the same near-death
moment, they would naturally want to come together. They
could find a shoulder to lean on during the emotional
upheaval, or a friend to hug during each new moment of
relief and exultation.*

*Glenn colorfully walks me through the landscape of this new
Flight 1549 community. As you read his account, consider
where you can build more community to sustain you. It may
well be that if we lose connection with a sense of community, we
will start to lose connection with the very essential nature of
being human. Wherever we are and whatever we've been
through, we can look around for those who share our values,
our interests, our hopes and dreams. And then we can step into
that community and make it our own. Notice that Glenn offers
an important secondary lesson: when you embrace a new community, don't be afraid to bring along who you really are.*

—Kevin

In Glenn's Words

IT WAS THE FIRST REUNION of Flight 1549 passengers and
Captain Sullenberger, and I was on a mission. With a blank

journal, I walked the ballroom of the Westin Hotel in Charlotte, asking all my fifty or so fellow passengers who had turned out for the filming of the *60 Minutes* segment to autograph it. I made sure to get Sully to sign and since Katie Couric was there to conduct the interviews, I approached her, too.

"It's for my three kids," I explained. "I'm going to put together a whole box of Flight 1549 memorabilia. I've got my Red Cross blanket and sweatshirt, too."

Gaining the personal signatures of the courageous souls whom I shivered and stood with on the Hudson River on January 15 was also very much for me. As I told an interviewer that day, this was my flight crash family, my new buddy group. As Sully would say on his first major interview on *60 Minutes*, we would be forever linked in our hearts and minds. I wanted a tangible reminder.

"Hey, you've got to do this over," I chided one passenger who had signed in small, inconspicuous letters. "Sign it big, like a rock star! And don't forget to add your seat number."

By now, some of the passengers were getting to know me as the guy with the persistent and maybe offbeat sense of humor. I made sure Sully and Katie knew it, too. When Katie entered the ballroom to brief us on Sully's impending entry, I blurted out, "Hey, Katie, when you see Dan Rather tell him hello for me."

"We really don't talk very much," she said in a composed manner before turning to another passenger and asking, "So, is that the class clown?"

When it was my turn to greet Sully in the reception line, I introduced myself as "the guy knocking on your door after you made that 'brace for impact' announcement, to ask if you needed any help in there."

"Well, I appreciated that," Sully said, still showing that unflappable demeanor.

After I had collected more than a dozen signatures, another passenger approached me. "You should get on the e-mail distribution list of passengers," he said. "You'll get a bunch more people to sign your book."

What an idea! I contacted the fellow who had launched the e-mail list, and he showed me the current roster of twenty or thirty passengers. Having a bunch of new names to e-mail got me thinking. What if we added our home addresses so I could send everyone on my flight a Christmas card? And how about phone numbers so we might surprise someone directly with a call? What if we included our seat numbers so we might learn the name of that man or woman who yanked us out of the Hudson, or kept us steady on the wing, or said just the right thing to keep us sane during some crazy moment of the crash and rescue? Now we'd have a way to track them down and thank them personally. Oh, and thinking of the rescue, what if we also mentioned which ferry picked us up and whether we were taken to the New York or New Jersey side of the Hudson?

Why stop there? We also could add a category to name the location where each person spent the night of January 15: one of the New York area hotels; with nearby friends or family; or, for the hearty souls, making it home to Charlotte or other destinations. Oh, and since we're tracking them home, shouldn't we have a place for each passenger to list the names of significant others and children, if they chose to?

I shared all my ideas with the founder of the e-mail list, and before long I found myself in charge of collecting all this data and distributing the passenger list to everyone on it. As I laid it all out on an Excel spreadsheet, I said to one new passenger friend, "Isn't this more fun than getting your class-mates to sign your high school yearbook?" With word of mouth, the list rapidly swelled: 25, 30, 40, 50, 60. Within weeks we were up to about half of the 150 passengers and still growing.

"Are you working on that list *again*?" my wife, Ann Marie, laughed one night.

"Just a sec, honey," I said. "I'm doing the demographics: got to know how many passengers from Charlotte, how many from New York, Massachusetts, Tennessee. . . . Did you know we had two from Colorado? Oh, and one from the state of Washington?"

We were beginning to put together the full roster of entire rows or even sections of the plane. When a new passenger would come "on list," he or she would often send me a sin-cere thank-you: "I'm so glad you're doing this, Glenn. I have wanted to reach out, but I only knew one or two of the other passengers." Or: "I am so grateful that I found the name of the man who pulled me out of the river and got me back on the wing when I slipped!" Often the newbie would share his or her brief crash story, or confide to the group a struggle with the emotional ups and downs, or the common fear of being on a plane again. We were part support group, part extended family.

Other outreach efforts sprang up. Vicki Barnhardt launched the "1549 Survivors" group on Facebook, and when she asked me to serve as one of the administrators there, I was happy to step in. Then, when some distribution list members expressed concern with the flood of e-mails circulating among our growing community, and a few outsiders tried to crash our party, Darren Beck suggested we branch out to a Yahoo! group. There, we could more effectively monitor the influx of new members and manage the flow of communication. The private Yahoo! entity soon became the group of record for Flight 1549 passengers. I was not at all offended. Once our distribution list had topped the one hundred mark, it was becoming a bit unwieldy. Anyway, Darren also invited me to coadministrate that new group, which I was equally happy to do.

I was getting a reputation as group organizer, and I loved it. I didn't even mind when some passengers would say, "That Glenn, he's kind of kooky." I just wasn't sure why they would think that, unless it was the drink I created and served at one of our first social gatherings of passengers in Charlotte. I called it the "Brace for Impact" and it had three parts bourbon, to honor the strong contingent of Southerners on the plane; one part Irish Mist, to acknowledge the New York Irish cops and firemen from the rescue; and a splash of bitters for that stom-

ach upset *some* passengers may have experienced just before
Sully brought us down on Hudson runway number one.

Or maybe they were within earshot on crash day at Pier
78, one of the rescue landing areas, when I looked around at
the growing ranks of first responders and dignitaries and
shouted out, "So where's the mayor? Like he could have
someplace more important to be today?" When Mayor
Bloomberg actually did arrive, I didn't miss a beat. "Hey,
Mayor, can I have those sterling cufflinks you're wearing?
They'd make a great memento for the day," I said. When he
humphed something about not being able to part with my
coveted prize and pulled out one of those Big Apple pins, I
quipped, "You've got hundreds of these that you're handing
out like candy." Seeing the humor in the moment, the mayor
placed the pin in my hand and said, "Now don't go selling
this on eBay."

Humor is just part of who I am. I'm the friend who greets
old pals by reciting the best lines from *Caddyshack*, and the
kind of dad who loves watching reruns of *SpongeBob* and *The
Fairly OddParents* as much as my sons, Sean, Brett, and Ryan,
do. Growing up in Clifton, New Jersey, my brother Craig and
I would secretly stay up late studying all the routines on com-
edy improv shows and go to sleep laughing.

I don't share this with everyone, but after the crash I
understood that I would never be the same person again. It's
just like you won't get your old life back after a parent dies
or after your first child is born. You just won't. It's hard to
explain. I see one example now in how I relate to politics. I

love politics. It's fun, a great way to stir up conversation. It can provide food for the mind. But I used to be very vehement in my views and would be the first to share them in any gathering of family, friends, or coworkers. Now I find myself holding back and just listening to what other people say. I understand that if I want to add something of value, it's better to have more information first. Sometimes I don't say anything. When I watch the political discourse around us, I don't have the stomach for the venomous stream of hatred from both sides anymore. I just don't think you accomplish anything by taking one viewpoint and trying to drag everyone along. A better way to resolve our problems is through collective reasoning.

I'm even different in helping my kids with their homework. Before, if they were struggling with a math problem I'd be quick to say, "That's not so good; this is a better way to get it done." Now I recognize that there's more creativity to it. If they take a more circuitous route to get to Point B, that's fine. They don't have to follow my way of how to solve the problem.

So I'm changing, and it's taken time. And I decided that whatever was going to be different with the new Glenn, I wanted to keep something important from the old Glenn. So I'm still kooky. Of course, I'm less cutting with my remarks to my fellow passengers because I know how vulnerable many of them are. And the truth is, I can be a bit vulnerable under the jokes, too. Humor is a part of who I am, but it's not all of me.

The organizing of passengers is part of the old Glenn, too. When we moved from a hamlet of a neighborhood in Jersey to a community on a golf course in Charlotte six years ago, I said to myself, "I've got to find some way to get people together here." So my wife and I took our chairs from Dick's Sporting Goods and plopped them near the end of our drive-way every night and waited. After a couple of nights of strange looks, a few folks stopped by to say hi and then a few more. Soon most of our neighbors started coming around and we'd be cutting up over beer and snacks while the kids frol-icked on the cul-de-sac.

That's the spirit I try to bring to the community of Flight 1549 passengers. We plan social events and gatherings of groups large and small. We have one-on-one and group dis-cussions on Yahoo! We meet each other for coffee or drinks. Wherever I travel, I try to arrange a visit with a passenger. Since my brother Craig and his friend Tommy helped gather me up from the pier the night of the crash, when I came up to New York I got them together with first responder Scott Koen and gave my brother one of the challenge coins Scott created as keepsakes for the Hudson River miracle. And I recently got together with Brad Wentzell for a barbecue.

We really do seem like family, even the ones I may not want to spend forty minutes with, or they with me. But it's funny how that one passenger you might be willing to embrace but don't think you'd like slowly becomes someone you *would* like to be with for forty minutes. When I get on a plane these days, I find myself thinking how usually you don't expect to ever see the people on board with you again. This is different. What we're doing is important, maybe not save-the-world important but important to us. We're staying connected.

So as our first year as family draws near to a close, I will be sending out those Christmas cards to every passenger I can find from all the lists. I've got something funny in mind, but I'm not going to tell. But you can bet that come December I'll be monitoring the Flight 1549 Yahoo! group and the 1549 Survivors Facebook group to see what they say about what kooky Glenn did now.

20
Bill Zuhoski:
TRUSTING YOURSELF

Trust yourself. You know more than you think you do.

—Benjamin Spock, MD

Bill Zuhoski *is aware he doesn't fit the profile of most of the passengers you may have heard about from Flight 1549. Though he lives on Long Island, it's way out on the eastern part and he does not work in New York City. He's not a business executive or high-level sales manager. He services swimming pools. He has no military experience and no children of his own. He's single, and he was just twenty-three on the day of the crash. He doesn't rely on air travel for his job, and he could probably count with his fingers how many times he has flown at all.*

He's not bothered at all that he may be different in some surface ways from many of his fellow passengers. It's just something he has noticed from media reports and some of the Flight 1549 group contact. He knows about the six golfing buddies on the plane, of course, and as you'll see from his account, he certainly has something in common with them. I also fill him in on twenty-something passenger Michele Davis from Olympia, Washington. But as we talk

I'm thinking mostly of what Bill does share with many other folks on the plane that day. At the moment of the crash, when he had to quickly decide what he needed to do, he followed his instincts. He trusted his experience, trusted himself.

For any of us caught in a trauma, emergency, or just a trying time, that's not always easy to do. We panic. We grope for answers. We feel lost. Not Bill. In his own unique way, he was following his lived experience in the same way that a military leader like Mark Hood followed his. Bill's experience is different, and his actions driven by instinct were different, born in large part from growing up in a large and close family. As it turned out, his choices on the Hudson weren't critical—but they sure might have been. And he was ready. You will soon learn how this was true. You'll also learn about how Bill's father trusted his own instincts after the crash and what he was stirred to do. As you read, you might ask yourself if there is any area in your own life where you have not been fully honoring your own lived experience. Is there some situation where you need to trust yourself more? You might be surprised about how turning your attention to what you have lived through, and how your instincts and self-trust guided you, may provide important answers for what you need to do, and where you need to go today.

—Kevin

In Bill's Words

I DON'T KNOW HOW the whole idea started. I'm not sure who dared whom, or where we might have heard about others crazy enough to do it. All I know is it began when I was still a kid, and we kept it up until a couple of years after my older brother Michael finished high school.

Here's the routine: Once a month, Michael, myself, and my younger brother Brian would go down to Beachcombers Beach near our home in Cutchogue, on eastern Long Island, and take a dip in the Long Island Sound. I mean once *every* month, including November, December, January, February—you get the picture. When the designated day arrived, it didn't matter how cold it was. We would run down the hill from our house at full speed, peel off our clothes down to our bathing suits, dive right in, and stay in that water long enough to call it a real swim. Then we'd charge back home with shrieks of pain and joy, and jump into a hot shower. We didn't have a name for ourselves, though if you were to call us the Young Polar Bears we probably would not have objected.

When Michael got old enough to get his driver's license, we cheated a little. Michael would drive us down to the beach and keep the car running, the heat cranked all the way up, while we went into the water. Then we'd hightail it back to the car and warm up before heading home.

Over the years, the shock of that first contact with the freezing water began to wear off. I got used to it, almost. I was around water most of the time anyway, working as a lifeguard for a couple of summers and then getting a job selling and servicing swimming pools. I was a good swimmer, and I paid attention to the conditions and environment wherever I found myself.

Of course, not everything we did was related to water. I grew up in a large and close extended family, with forty or more cousins within ten minutes of us. When I was young, my grandparents ran a potato farm. They also grew corn, which we loved to cook and eat right off the stalks. Just before dark, my brothers, cousins, and I would play "Man Hunt," hiding in those tall stalks until somebody found you. My grandparents passed the farm on to my uncle, and come about Thanksgiving, he turns it into a tree nursery, with a cut-your-own option for Christmas tree shoppers. I work there during the holiday season, along with winter construction I do with my dad to keep me going when no one is doing much with swimming pools.

Christmas means dozens of relatives celebrating together. We also have major Fourth of July family barbecues and New Year's Eve parties at J&Rs Steak House, where we pretty much close the place down. To me, large parties with family are much better than big gatherings with friends. Half the people at a friend's party you usually don't want to talk to or even be around, but I never feel that way when our family gets together.

It always seemed like we were pretty lucky when it came to accidents. I remember the time when Michael was about seventeen, and he was out late at night and just maybe driving a bit too fast. His car smashed into a telephone pole. My uncle Steven, a cop in a nearby town, brought him home with nothing worse than cuts and bruises. I don't know what might have been said between my brother and father in private, but when my dad turned to me, he just said, "Learn from this guy!"

When I was still too young to drive, I was coming home from soccer practice at Mattituck High School when the car my friend was driving got hit by a drunk driver. My friend and I both smacked into the windshield. "Mom, call 911," I said when I managed to get out my phone. "We've been in an accident right up the road."

"Oh, come on, Bill," she said. "You know, you shouldn't joke about things like that."

"Um, Mom, I'm not joking. We're bleeding pretty good here. You might want to come down."

In fact, my friend was cut up bad enough to require reconstructive surgery. I got off with ten or twelve stitches. Another friend, Dan, was in the backseat that day and didn't get hurt at all. We stayed friends through high school and beyond. It was Dan I was headed to visit on January 15. He lived in Myrtle Beach, and we were going to get together for a little golf and a lot of winter rest and play.

I actually had been scheduled on a morning flight out of LaGuardia on Spirit Airlines that day, but when my flight was canceled due to early-morning snow, I was booked on US Airways Flight 1549. I would not find out until much later that the same thing happened to a group of friends from

Massachusetts going to Myrtle Beach for a golf vacation. I didn't know them, but maybe we will meet someday.

I was seated in 23E, and as you might have heard from the media, I became known as the Naked Passenger. In a nutshell, here's what happened:

I usually wear contacts when I travel but that morning I was too lazy to put them in. So I was wearing my glasses. Can't see a foot in front of me without them. When our rear section absorbed the worst impact of Sully's brilliant landing, I hit my head on the seat in front of me. My glasses flew off. With water quickly pouring in up to my waist, there was no way I was going to find them. But I didn't need glasses to realize how deep the water was rising and how fast.

You're going to have to swim here, maybe a long way, in the plane and maybe in the river, I thought. Just keeping aware of the conditions. Instinctively, I stripped off my jeans, T-shirt, buttondown shirt and shoes—all the way down to my boxers. All I could think of was that this would help me swim faster and farther. That's what it might take to survive. And we never went in with all our clothes in January on the Long Island Sound.

Then, a second thought: *You're going to have to get to dry space right now, or you're dead right here.* I'm a runner and a pretty good athlete, so I just started climbing over all the rows of seats in front of me. I didn't know the side exit doors were open, with people standing on the wings, because I couldn't see far enough to notice them. I just kept climbing all twenty-three rows until I got to the front and stumbled my way to the life raft.

On the ferry a while later, I sat huddled in blankets. I didn't have to swim for it, after all.

"Weren't you afraid of getting hypothermia—you know, without your clothes on?" someone asked me.

"Nah," I said, with half a grin. "I'm kind of used to cold water."

I didn't explain about those winter swims in Long Island Sound. I was just doing what I thought I had to do. Instinct, I guess.

When I called home on a phone a cop loaned me, my younger sister answered. "Theresa, is anybody else home?" I asked. "No, Dad's out and Mom took her class on a field trip," she responded. I found out later that Mom's class had gone to the Metropolitan Museum of Art, just blocks from where we went down. "Never mind, I'll call back," I said. I didn't want to worry her. No one in my family had any reason to believe I would have been on this afternoon flight.

At St. Luke's Hospital, where I still couldn't see a foot in front of me, I managed to borrow another phone and finally got through to my father on his cell.

"Dad, did you see the news about that plane that crashed in the Hudson? My flight got canceled and I was on that plane . . . but I'm okay," I said. "Do you think you and Brian could come in and pick me up at St. Luke's Hospital?"

"We're heading your way right now!" he shouted. "Be there in less than an hour."

Less than an hour? That meant he had been on the road for at least sixty minutes already! "Dad, how did you know?" I asked. "I wasn't even supposed to be on that flight."

"When I heard the news, I just called Michael and said 'I think Bill was on that plane!' I just had a feeling, a bad feeling."

I guess when you're part of a large, close-knit family, sometimes you do know. Even if you can't explain how or why.

When they all got to the hospital, my dad greeted me with a bear hug. "You gave us the scare of our lives," he said. It was the first time my dad had hugged me in, oh, ten years or more. Among the males of my family, as close as we are, we are just not huggers. We're guys. But in the next forty-eight hours I hugged uncles I'm not sure I had ever hugged, and when my grandfather wrapped his arms around me he actually wept—something else you don't see the Zuhoski males do.

When I got home, the newspapers called. "If I knew I was going to be rescued so fast, I would have kept my pants on," I told them.

That was all six months ago. I never did make it down to Myrtle Beach. A few days after the crash, I turned down a chance to fly, all expenses paid, to Los Angeles to appear on *The Ellen DeGeneres Show*. I still have not flown since the crash, and I do not plan to. I know the odds against anything like that happening again are huge, but the way I figure it is that if I was in a plane and something like that did happen again, what are the odds of surviving it again? I took a bus to Atlantic City a while ago and even that got me a little freaked out. And, since I'm being really honest here, I get antsy riding in a car or pickup, unless I'm at the wheel. I just don't like that feeling of being out of control.

I'm okay around the water, though. Some things don't change.

I don't think about Flight 1549 much, but not long ago we got our recovered belongings back from US Airways. I didn't get my glasses, or my shoes, but when I reported the $700 in cash (Myrtle Beach vacation money) missing from my wallet, I was amazed that they gave me the money back. I'm taking it to Mohegan Sun (a Connecticut casino).

The big family get-togethers are still going strong. Not long ago we all converged for my grandparents' sixtieth wedding anniversary. We went to Mass together, ate a big meal out together, and then streamed into my aunt's house. There was a moment there when I was looking at the cake as my grandparents were about to cut it, I glanced around the room at the faces of my uncles and cousins, and maybe I kinda, sorta cried for a second.

But let's be clear about one thing. There have been no more hugs with my dad or my brothers since the fifteenth of January. It would take another plane crash for that to happen.

P.S. The surprises and good fortune in the aftermath of Flight 1549 have continued for Bill. One October morning, after a night at that same casino he had headed to with his reimbursed vacation money, Bill received a phone call. A drawing had been held as part of a promotional night while he had been playing, and Bill had won first prize: $10,000!

REFLECTIONS

Our way is not soft grass, it's a mountain path with lots of rocks. But it goes upward, forward, forward, toward the sun.

—Dr. Ruth Westheimer

Whatever form our life lessons take, we are given the opportunity to learn from them ... or pretend they didn't happen. So many moments come our way carrying a message that tells us something important. Whether it is a beautiful sunset that reminds us of that which is larger than we are, or the connection with a friend or family member that offers us the deep lessons of love, life is always our teacher. Sometimes the lessons are gentle and joyous, sometimes painful and frightening. *What are the lessons that are right there for us?*

We are all students, and we all learn, slowly or quickly, some of what is truly important. Our passengers and first responders had that rare opportunity to learn huge lessons, and so they have. These lessons have not always come easily, though. There has been, for them, as there is for all of us, pain, loss, and fear, and these wounds have led to healing and growth in deep and profound ways.

For some, the lessons of this plane crash reminded them of what they already knew. For others, new lessons came with the plane crash. Matt has taken a firm hold of what he's learned from this accident. In part he's been able to do this because what he learned resonated with everything he already knew, things he was taught, ways he wanted to be. And now his work is to live these lessons, just as Sully did in those crucial few moments over the Hudson. Don, on the other hand, opened up doors to his own vulnerability in a way that has brought him face-to-face with fear and has moved him into closer connections with family, friends, colleagues, strangers, and God.

For every passenger and for all of us, the lessons are available, even when they are not dramatic. And in learning, we can heal. As Maryann noted, survival is more than staying alive. And so we ask, consciously or unconsciously: *how do I live my life fully?* No one makes it through life without a fair number of very difficult experiences of fear, sadness, and grief. This is the human condition. Our greatest challenge is to keep growing and to find a way to thrive, even in the face of life events that are challenging. We are all survivors. We are resilient, even when wounded. We are courageous, even facing death. The human spirit is strong and our invitation is to stay the course. And that means holding both our strengths and our weaknesses as part of the truth of who we are. For wholeness includes both strength and vulnerability. And all of us are vulnerable. Somewhere we all know that, though we may try not to notice.

As we come to know ourselves in our wholeness, in our courage and in our fear, in our strength and in our vulnerability, we connect more deeply than ever to our human family. Our community is large. It may start with our friends and family but extends to our world. Finding those connections helps us all heal. For when we look around, we see others just like us. We see people with magnificent gifts—some that shine publicly for all to see, some that simply glimmer in the quiet of their world. And we see people who have been hurt—by life, trauma, passing problems, and the normal changing nature of life, in which some days we are up and some days we are down.

Every one of us is both the healer and the one who needs to be healed. Inevitably, we will play both roles over and over in our lives. And so it should be. Each of us will find times when we are the helper and times when we need to be helped. How could it be otherwise? Sometimes we need professional help, whether to fix our car or help heal our own inner pain. Sometimes life helps us, by its very nature. Sometimes our best friend, spouse, parent, or child pitches in to give us a hand. Sometimes the friendly smile of a stranger is all we need. And as often as we are helped, we help. We are the friend, the family member, the stranger, the caring other who lends a hand to help someone else.

For all, our passengers and ourselves, learning the lessons that life teaches us is the path of healing. And these lessons, while unique for each person, will share many elements. They will be about trusting ourselves, being authentic, allowing our feelings, reaching out to others in love and caring . . . and in need. These lessons will take us through every twist and turn of life. And it is our job to notice the lesson. Big or small, hard or easy, when we take in what life is teaching, we learn those most valuable lessons that help us become the best we can be. *What is life teaching me today?*

Part IV
Sharing the Gift

Caring about others, running the risk of feeling, and leaving an impact on people, brings happiness.

—Rabbi Harold S. Kushner

21
Beth McHugh:
HUGGING LIKE YOU MEAN IT

*Millions and millions of years would still not give
me half enough time to describe that tiny instant of
all eternity when you put your arms around me and
I put my arms around you.*

—Jacques Prévert

*Ever since she was lifted out of the cold, cold Hudson
River, Beth has been hugging everyone she knows and
everyone she meets. It's one of the many touching stories
that have emerged since the crash, and I had heard about it
before I met Beth at a Charlotte hotel where she was being
interviewed for the new NBC Weekend TODAY segment
"Second Chances." But knowing about this ritual adopted
by one of the survivors of Flight 1549 is very different from
seeing it. As you read Beth's story, you will learn what I
witnessed.*

*Beth is a thoughtful and articulate woman, and she's
been thinking a lot about these hugs. Why she feels called
to hug everyone. Why even strangers so willingly open their
arms to her. What is being communicated in those hugs.
What hugs can bring to her life, to their lives, and maybe*

even to the world. She certainly provides us food for thought about who we need to hug, or to be hugged by, and how we might become more fully engaged in the act of hugging so that we are really hugging life!

There's something else to consider: what old feelings or beliefs might we need to let go of to fully hug, to fully love, to fully live? For Beth it might have been, at least in part, an old fear. As a child she had dreams and images of riding in her family car when it shot off some bridge and plunged into the river below. The fear was so embedded that as an adult she wouldn't buy cars with electric windows. She insisted on crank-style windows; she had to be able to get out. Of course her car never did go into a river, but her plane did. But she didn't drown in that frigid Hudson. She lived! How could she not want to hug?

—Kevin

In Beth's Words

"DO YOU ALL KNOW how it feels to hug someone when you really mean it?"

I asked that question to about 250 young people at Clover High School near my home in Lake Wylie, South Carolina. I could tell from their faces that some of them did know, and some didn't. The truth is, I'm not sure I fully knew what it felt like to hug this way before the Hudson River Miracle.

Of course, I'd hugged before. We all have. After growing up

in a family of thirteen siblings, when it sometimes seemed we never had enough of anything, I made sure to give my own three daughters plenty of hugs every day I was with them. But there are hugs, and there are *hugs!*

It began when I arrived at my daughter Caitlin's house in New Jersey after I left the hospital late on the night of the crash. The second we met, we just held on to each other for a long time. I mean, a *really* long time.

> *Recalls Caitlin, who hugged her mom after handing her three-month-old baby, Jack, to her husband Mark: "I cried harder than I had all day. I was struck by how fragile she looked. She was wearing these New York Waterway pants two feet too long and that big black sweater. She was a mess. I don't know how long we hugged but finally I said, "Mom, I'm never letting you leave again."'*
>
> *Daughter Megan arrived early the next afternoon after driving up from Charlottesville, Virginia. "I was afraid she was still freezing from that cold, cold water, so I just wrapped my arms around her tight," relates Megan. "I felt her sigh, like that sound when you first let air out of an air mattress."*
>
> *Beth later visited her daughter Kyran in upstate New York. "I thought I had worked through the emotions," she says, "but when I saw her coming down the Jetway I was surprised by the intensity of my feelings and of the hugs."*

There was something in all those first family hugs that meant more than hugs had ever meant before. Glancing at my high school audience that day, I saw that they too began to feel this invitation to be moved, to be really held. I noticed some tears. Not something you often see in a roomful of fifteen- to eighteen-year-olds.

I had begun my talk with the story of the crash. Everyone wants to hear it. Young or old, male or female, everyone tries to imagine what it would feel like to be sitting in that eerie silence of our airplane hovering below the skyscrapers. I said every prayer I could think of. I prayed to God and my guardian angels. I prayed to Daddy, and to my mother and grampa, who all have passed away. I was about to realize my worst childhood fear. "I hope you're there waiting for me, Daddy," I prayed, "and please don't let me stay in the water too long."

"But that bad dream didn't come true," I told these youngsters in the audience.

Next I shared the story of our stunning rescue, and of course they loved the part about how someone had to push my butt up the Jacob's ladder onto the ferry. "Damn," I said to myself, "if only I had lost those forty pounds, this would be a lot easier."

Then I went on to tell them more about me . . . and other people and hugs. After those melting hugs with my family, I made a vow: from then on, I would hug every person with whom I shared more than a brief encounter. Anyone. Anywhere. Anytime. I've kept to that vow ever since. I don't know why, but it feels as if my miracle is somehow extended through each and every hug. I look at each person I meet as someone I would never have known—a gift to me. I hope that I too can be a gift to them.

I got started before my flight home just days after the crash. When I stopped to fill my rental car with gas near the airport, I could tell from the turban and the voice that the attendant was of Middle Eastern descent. I thought, *What are the proper cultural boundaries here?* But a commitment was a commitment. He spotted my NY Waterway sweatshirt and asked, "Were you one of the rescuers of that plane crash in the Hudson?"

I shook my head and said, "No, I was one of the passengers."

Smiling broadly, he said, "That was truly God's blessing."

Of course it had been a miracle, God's blessing. But how do you ask a man you've never met, a total stranger, to hug you?

"I was wondering if . . . we can exchange a hug?" I finally said.

He hesitated and looked at me. Then he leaned over, reached out with his hand and lightly touched my cheek. And then he slowly and carefully touched my other cheek. In my tears I understood: connections are possible with anyone, anywhere.

At Newark Airport I was required to go through extra screening because I didn't have any ID. Of course I didn't! It was all in the Hudson. I had an escort from the airline who explained who I was, and that helped, but the woman in security told me that rules were rules. She still had to pat me down.

"You okay?" she asked, in a still formal tone. She had heard the story from the airline escort.

"Oh, I'm fine. . . . It's just that now I know you so I have to hug you. But I certainly understand the strict rules you must have here so—"

"Honey," she said, "bring it on!" And after a hug that lasted longer than it takes some teenagers to wolf down two Big Macs, she said, "I feel like I've just hugged a miracle."

At home, a floral delivery man pulled up, and we spoke long enough for me to explain why I was getting so many flowers. Here we go, a new connection! "Can I give you a hug?" I asked.

He leaned right in for his hug, and on his way back to the van he said, "I can't wait to tell my wife I've met you! She's been watching the news for days on TV." Then he ran back up the steps and gave me another hug.

I thought about what was happening. Hugging is all about celebrating life. Maybe that's what these strangers were feeling. Life is a gift. Plus, a hug doesn't cost anything. It takes hardly any time. It benefits both parties. And it may be the only hug that person gets that day.

I take my hugging onto airplanes with me. Sometimes I wind up on that same 2:45 PM Thursday flight from LaGuardia to Charlotte after working with clients in New York and New Jersey, and, yes, I do feel the fear when we go over the Hudson. It helps that loved ones ask their guardian angels to watch over me, but when I get on board, I introduce myself to the flight attendants as a Flight 1549 survivor. I ask politely if I can speak to the pilot, and they always say yes. In the cockpit, I tell my story.

"We sit back there and have no control over what happens up here and usually don't pay attention," I tell them. "But I will never take you for granted again. We entrust you with our lives, and you are doing a great job at keeping us safe."

As the pilot and copilot thank me, they say, "We hardly ever hear this message." Then they ask me about the crash, and of course we don't finish until the hugs. Back in the cabin the flight attendants usually ask me more questions, and they get their hugs, too. "You should come to our safety training sessions. We need to hear the passengers' stories," one flight attendant told me. And maybe I will.

As Beth continues our interview while having lunch at that Charlotte hotel, a waitress approaches and boldly asks Beth if she is writing a book about her life. When Beth explains, the waitress says, "I don't believe it! My cousin was supposed to be on that flight." Their lively exchange ends with a hug, as does the long interaction with the female native of Colombia who had escorted Beth to the restaurant. Beth even hugs the NBC cameraman who tells her that she has given him much to think about each time he steps onto a plane. Each person's eyes light up in the moment of the hug.

The hugging just keeps feeding me. I don't see it stopping. Now I find myself paying more attention to the spirit behind these hugs, the qualities and feelings that guide me in going forward with my renewed life and that perhaps may speak to others. Here are four key ones:

1. **Acceptance:** After those first terrifying seconds when I could see that we were gliding quickly downward, below the tops of the New York City skyscrapers, that

we couldn't get to an airport, that we had no engine power, that we were over water, I took a breath. "So this is how it's going to happen," I said to myself as I began to pray. I had reached acceptance. Then, somehow, what actually happened was not at all what I had expected.

When any of us can find that place of acceptance, we have taken a huge step. You get up, and it's a new day every day. You will face challenges and you can either accept them or not, and if you can accept them, they can become less daunting, more workable. You can accept people for who they are, what they are, and how they live. You become more tolerant.

2. **Hope:** Everything I have seen and felt since Flight 1549 reminds me that miracles generate hope. That's why so many people have been drawn to this story. Hope helps us get up every day. We have a sense that we can go to work, we can raise our children, and even if we face something as bad as cancer, maybe we can get through the awful treatment and feel better and continue living.

Hope tells us that there's something better out there, something to strive for. It helps us take chances: to start a business, to get married, to have a child. And even as we mourn other terrible disasters that do not have the ending we were so blessed to have, we keep looking for miracles. We go on searching for hope that there can be another way.

3. **Gratitude:** When I settled into that rescue ferry on the Hudson, I kept saying to myself silently, "We're alive!

We're alive!" I don't practice any organized religion, but I am a spiritual being, and that was a deeply spiritual moment, a dramatic experience of gratitude. I had to learn gratitude early. I grew up in the late 1940s and early '50s on a farm in rural Missouri with no running water, no electricity, no indoor plumbing. Still, we had cows and pigs to sustain us, a home to live in . . . and love. Our Christmas presents often came from Goodwill. For the girls, that might be a new dress for an old doll. At thirteen, I went to work as a nurse's aide, bathing and feeding nine or ten infants in a hospital nursery. As students at the Catholic school, we had to wear the same white blouse, white socks, and navy blue uniform every day. We learned gratitude.

When we practice gratitude, we can wake up and say, "Thank you for this beautiful day!" Even if it's raining it's still beautiful. When I'm at an airport, and I hear people grumble about a flight delay, I want to tell them, "A delay is time to think, to reflect." If we all stop to notice things to be grateful for, we realize we probably have hundreds of them.

4. **Kindness:** Among the countless acts of simple human kindness I witnessed that day on the Hudson, one stands out. On the ferry, a young woman noticed my soaking feet and offered me her socks. "No, you keep them, or you'll be cold," I said, to which she responded, "But I have boots." So I put on those soft black socks, still warm from her skin. I've kept those socks and still wear them.

I think of her often, and wish I could hug her.

How would it change our lives if everyone were kinder than necessary? You never know when that person beside you is having a terrible day and that's all they need. When you practice kindness, you just naturally care more for other people and feel more connected to the greater whole. Like that movie *Pay It Forward*, when I do something for someone and the other person asks, "How can I ever repay you?" I answer, "Don't try. Do something for someone else. Pass it on."

Back at Clover High School, I was finishing my talk. "There's something else these hugs do," I said. "They are a way of leaving echoes. That's something I would urge all of you to find a way to do in your lives. Let people know who you are, that you've been here in this life and you have made a difference. Oh, one more thing. I will stand by this podium when I'm done and share a hug with any of you who would like one."

The line reached halfway up the aisles. Lots of the girls cried. But you want to know who gave some of the longest, heartiest, and most sincere hugs? The big, strapping football types, to whom I was probably much more the image of their grandmother than some cute young woman they would rather hug!

That's the kind of response that tells me I've got a lot more hugs in me yet.

22
Dave Sanderson:
SPEAKING FROM THE HEART

When pure sincerity forms within, it is outwardly realized in other people's hearts.

—Lao Tze

It was a few months after the crash. Dave Sanderson was sorting through his mail and came across a package from New York City. Recognizing the name on the return address, he smiled and eagerly opened it. It was from Tess, the mom on the plane with her husband, her young daughter, and her baby. "Thank you for helping to save our family's lives," she had written. As Dave relives that poignant moment from the Hudson, I see his eyes open wider, his face brighten. A fellow passenger has shared something from her heart and it has touched his heart. Thank you. It's what each of the passengers have been saying to one another and to everyone who helped save their lives on January 15, and they all deeply mean it. Dave will tell you that what he did in helping this young mother, which he describes in his story, was just a small part of what steered her and her baby to safety. Many others pitched in, too. It was that way all over the plane, and in the frigid *water. Everyone stepped up. A helping hand or calming voice, usually more than one at a time, emerged at every step, every stroke, every tear. Each time Dave and so many other passengers relate this, I more fully appreciate that circuit of thanks as a beautiful thing.*

I wonder if that's what Dave takes with him up there on the podium when he talks about the Miracle on the Hudson as a popular inspirational speaker. As he recounts his "Brace for Impact" story to audiences large and small, I suspect he's saying thank you: thank you to God, thank you to Sully, thank you to the rescue personnel, thank you to the Red Cross, thank you to his fellow passengers. The sentiment comes directly from his heart, and it goes right into the hearts of others. That's why he keeps getting invited to speak. Six months after the crash, he co-organized a thank-you event with Barry Leonard at the Palisades Medical Center on the New Jersey shore of the Hudson to express gratitude toward hospital staff and all the Jersey first responders. Dave's experience is a reminder to us all: when we speak from our hearts about something that has stirred us, and we allow ourselves to relive it, to feel the gratitude behind it, we have a great capacity to touch, to uplift, and to inspire others. If we all lived from the heart in our little and our big actions, we too would be changing the world, one moment to the next, in each act of kindness, in every word from the heart.

—Kevin

In Dave's Words

I HAVE A CONFESSION TO MAKE. It's about the many public talks I have been honored to present about the Miracle on the Hudson. Sometimes I cry. I've choked back tears while getting ready to begin my presentation, welled up on stage while speaking, and sobbed while greeting attendees after I've finished.

The first time took me by surprise. I had been invited to speak to a men's group at my church, the Providence United Methodist Church in Charlotte. I was expecting the usual forty or fifty guys chowing down a few stacks of pancakes, but word had gotten around. By the time I got up to speak, there must have been 250 men *and* women there. "I see they ran out of food today," I laughed. "And you know what they say about Methodists—it's never a good idea to run out of food with us."

The icebreaker got people relaxed, and my talk, especially the part about our plane gliding closer and closer toward the Hudson in those final seconds before the crash, had them riveted. I went on to describe how God had to have been there with us at every stage: from Captain Sullenberger's heroic landing, to the time of day of the crash and rescue, to the rapid actions of the first responders, to the spirit of cooperation and selflessness of the passengers. It was not one miracle but many. "At every point in this flight, God intervened," I explained. "So if you don't believe in miracles or God, there are now one hundred fifty-five examples walking around the United States."

After my talk, I was surprised to see many people waiting

to approach me. One of them was a woman in her eighties, and though it appeared that she had been crying a few minutes earlier, she was wearing a warm smile as she seized my arm and leaned in close to me.

"I just want to tell you something," she said firmly, her voice just above a whisper. "Lately I have found myself questioning whether God really exists and if miracles really happen. Well, God bless you, young man, because now I believe in miracles."

As I looked in her eyes, I couldn't stop my own tears. "I have served today," I said to myself.

I've choked up many times since that moment. In March, I was invited to speak at the Scholarship and Endowment Luncheon at James Madison University (JMU), my alma mater. While I was waiting to go on, I looked around our table and made eye contact with a former JMU fraternity brother whom I had not seen since I graduated in 1983. *I might never have seen him again,* I thought. So there I was again, a forty-eight-year-old guy welling up in tears in public.

Fortunately, I regained my composure. Speaking at JMU was a special moment because my college had always been close to my heart. After growing up in southern Ohio and excelling in football, I flirted with the idea of attending Ohio State and trying to make the celebrated Buckeyes football team as a walk-on. But my mother, whom I always trusted, had a different idea. "Don't be a small fish in a big pond," she said.

So I chose JMU, my strong second choice, and after I tore up my knee and couldn't play football, I was grateful to be a part of the first graduating class in the school's international business program. After I had been in the working world as a single guy for a while, I was taking an aerobics class when a young woman noticed my JMU T-shirt. "Did you go to JMU?" she asked. "So did I!" That was the start of a relationship that has endured for twenty-two years of marriage and four great kids.

During my talk that day, I described the scene in the cabin after we landed. Seated toward the middle, I chose not to exit immediately, at first so as not to be trampled by passengers surging forward from the water-filled rear of the plane. Then I decided I should stay longer, to help people get out through our side exit door in as orderly a manner as possible. As I told the gathering at JMU that day, "Mom always told me that if you do the right thing, God will take care of you. The right thing to do that day was to get the women and children off first."

That meant helping Tess and her baby. When she reached the exit door, with many passengers waiting to get out behind her, I knew that if she stood on that water-covered wing she could slip and that baby could wind up in the Hudson in a heartbeat. So, with others assisting me, I helped direct her toward the life raft still wedged against the side of the plane and then asked what probably seemed like the impossible to any mom: toss her baby to passengers in the raft! I didn't want her to risk losing her footing and her grasp on her child on the way in. After some hesitation and the urging and assistance of a female passenger, Tess let go. Her baby was safe, and the line of passengers waiting behind her was able to proceed off the plane.

I wound up being the last or one of the last ones out of the rear of the cabin. By then, the wing on our side was precariously full, and so was the raft. I had nowhere to go. I wound up holding an awkward and vulnerable position with one foot on the wing and one foot still inside the plane. I also tried to reach out to the raft with one arm to help hold it steady alongside our floating jet. I was standing in water up to my waist for several minutes. When one of the first responders inadvertently bumped the plane as he prepared to take rescued passengers to the shore, I felt a splash of freezing water strike my back. Images of the Titanic plunging down in the icy waters flashed through my mind.

"I'm going to get sucked down under this water with the plane!" I told myself. So I leaped into the Hudson, setting course for one of the fast-approaching ferries. I was in that thirty-six-degree water for what seemed like several minutes more, and I thank my mom and dad for giving me swimming lessons as a boy or I never would have made it that far. Then, just as the last of the strength in my legs gave out, two men grabbed my arms and yanked me into the ferry. I don't even know who they were, but I call them two of my angels. Of course, I knew that my mom, who died in 1997, was my guardian angel all that day.

While paramedics treated me on the way to Palisades Medical Center on the Jersey side, I was told that my body temperature was dangerously low and my blood pressure dangerously high. I was at serious risk of a heart attack or stroke. When the hospital chaplain came to visit, I broke down in tears. But with excellent medical care, I was well enough to fly home the next day and go back to work the following Monday.

"All this—from the crash, to the rescue, to getting to the hospital—took only thirty minutes, about the time for a soap opera," I said that day at my alma mater. "Think about that. My whole life changed in those thirty minutes."

Sometimes the caring of those sponsoring my talks triggers my watery eyes. When I entered a Presbyterian church in nearby Gastonia, North Carolina, I looked up to see a blown-up copy of that stirring illustration from the *Sacramento Bee* of the hands of God holding up our plane. I was already on the verge of tears, and then, just before I was introduced, the organist played my grandmother's favorite hymn: "The Old Rugged Cross." The only thing that stopped my crying was getting the first few words out of my mouth.

Just before another event, two young boys approached me. "Miracle! Miracle Man!" one of them said with a beaming smile. Again I got moist eyes. Once, after a talk, I was struck by the sight of one of my daughter's friends coming up to shake my hand. This gentleman has courageously battled Lou Gehrig's disease. He was a battler, a survivor, too. Again, my floodgates opened.

Sometimes I find my eyes blinking or tearing while recalling images from the crash: the moment I held the cell phone loaned to me and punched out the number for Oracle, where I work as a sales manager. How close I had come to losing everything I had known in life.

The main consolation to breaking down during my talks is

knowing that the audience is crying more than I am. "Get your tissues out," warned Red Cross CEO and President Gail McGovern as she introduced me to the almost all-female national gathering of leading Red Cross donors through the Tiffany Circle, a society of women leaders and philanthropists. And they *did* cry. When I was done, making sure to mention how I had gone home from the crash wearing the sweatpants and sweatshirt the Red Cross had given me, they stood and cheered.

That event in Washington included a visit to Arlington National Cemetery, where I had lunch with two generals. On the bus back to the hotel, I met the wife of Neal Boortz, who insisted that I should be on her husband's nationally syndicated radio program that week. We also were escorted to the Supreme Court, where I was personally greeted by Justice Anthony M. Kennedy. I was so excited and so grateful for such opportunities! Early the next week I flew to Las Vegas, where I spoke at the Mirage Hotel to a gathering of more than a thousand human resource professionals. By the end of June, I had surpassed forty total speaking events.

My talks cover leadership, teamwork, crisis management, and faith, with different points of emphasis for different groups. After honoring the work of Sully Sullenberger, his crew, and the first responders, I point out that the survival of all 150 passengers would not have happened if all of us had not responded exactly as we did. In less than one minute, 150 people who mostly did not know one another, and probably didn't care to know one another, had to come together as a team. Imagine the potential of any company or group that responds to a crisis or challenge like that!

Speaking to hundreds of people was certainly not in my strategic life plan. But then I was never even supposed to be on Flight 1549. I only got on because a work meeting ended early. God put me in that seat for a reason. Perhaps part of it was my small role in helping my fellow passengers get off the plane safely, and part of it is embracing this new mission to share about it. This is my calling, and it comes with many rewards. I see every day how there is God's grace in the world. I see the goodness of people.

I have been blessed to have so many people encouraging me, including the folks at Oracle, and world acclaimed motivational speaker Tony Robbins. After attending one of Tony's seminars in San Diego in 1993, I was so inspired by his message that I contacted his office to volunteer. I've been assisting in security at Tony's live events ever since. As I would watch how Tony reached people, I would occasionally imagine what it might be like to inspire others with a message. But what was *my* message? With no clear answer, I focused on my success as a sales manager and on being a loving husband to Terri and devoted father to my four amazing kids: Chelsey, seventeen; Colleen, fifteen; Courtney, eleven; and Chance, my only son, seven.

January 15 gave me a message. I just take people inside this miracle and, as honestly as I can, share what I was thinking, feeling, doing, and wondering. I get up there without notes and look in their eyes, and I sense that I am connecting with their souls. Something happens to them in the hearing, and something always happens to me in the telling.

23

Hilda Roque-Dieguez, M.D.:
GIVING AND RECEIVING

We make a living by what we get, but we make a life by what we give.

—Winston Churchill

There are many unsung heroes in this miracle flight. We'll never know the names of most of them. From the first person who called 911; to the rescue boats; to passengers on the New York ferries who shared coats and phones and words of support; to families and friends who dropped their daily lives to be there for their loved ones. There was, Dr. Hilda Roque-Dieguez tells me, one young man on the New Jersey rescue site who gave his socks to a very cold passenger on the edge of hypothermia and frostbite. There was the sudden appearance, on both sides of the river, of clothing and blankets—in one case it was cooks' uniforms! There were the known helpers—the Red Cross, firefighters, police, emergency personnel—and the unknown ones. There was the amazing crew of Flight 1549, and there were the passengers, each a hero. Two states, joined by the Hudson River, came together to make this miracle possible. In this particular geographical area, right where the plane ditched, most of those involved shared a history of 9/11 that made them alert, that made them prepared, that made them all the more joyful when this event turned into a miracle, not a tragedy.

Talking to Hilda, I hear more about the event as she and the people she worked with that day experienced it. In the end they became another group of ordinary heroes: people who just did what they know how to do and saved lives doing it. She was one of the many unknown heroes, and that was fine with her. It is, after all, her life's work. When two passengers, Dave Sanderson and Barry Leonard, decided to put together a thank-you event for all those unsung heroes in July, Hilda got the appreciation she and so many others deserve. Being honored at a luncheon for all the New Jersey rescuers gave her goose bumps. "This is the greatest gift a doctor can receive," she said that day. But her appreciation lunch was cut short as she headed to the hospital to be there for her dad, the man who inspired her into the field of medicine. Talking to her on her lunch break during another busy day of healing, I was glad she had been noticed. Glad she had been thanked and honored. She deserves this.

—Dorothy

In Hilda's Words

I WAS BORN IN CUBA and my father was a physician. When we came here, I was about ten, and he continued his medical practice and has until very recently. Now he's taking care of my mom, who is ill. That's very hard for me. As a doctor I know how to help, but when it's your own mother and there's nothing you can do, that's really sad for me. I grew up around the idea that if someone needs help, you do what you can. This came from both my parents. They worked together. My mother was my father's support. She is strong and a people person. He is more shy. Their guidance helped to inspire me, both personally and in my profession. My brothers became doctors too. They're great. It's in our blood. In fact, when I became a doctor, I joined my father's practice, right here where I am now. How he and my mother lived and worked helped me become a better doctor. I don't think I could ever turn away from an emergency or from a person in need. I learned that in my family. But I lived it, first in 9/11 and then on January 15.

At the medical office that day, I was trying to get an ambulance for a seriously ill patient. The ambulances just weren't coming, and I was getting really annoyed. This was dangerous. And it was unusual not to get an immediate response. I was so scared and nervous, and no help was coming. I was really worried about the woman in my office, who might have stopped breathing at any moment. Finally, a young police officer came in. He was so tender, a young kid. "What's going on?" I asked, meaning why isn't the ambulance here.

"Don't you know what happened?" he asked.

I didn't, of course, because it was so early in the process and I wasn't watching the news. I was trying to save this woman! "You're kidding?" I said when he told me. "A plane in the Hudson?" "Yep. That's the story."

"Oh my God, Oh my God . . . ." I was loud and teary. "I can't believe this. This is not happening!" I ordered the young officer to take my patient to the hospital himself, for her safety and so I could get to the crash scene. I feel bad about that now, being so pushy, but he was so nice and I really needed his help.

I started pacing, telling people to close the office. This was a fight-or-flight reaction, and almost a flashback from 9/11. "We have to help," I kept saying. "Paula, we gotta go!"

She said, quietly, "I'll go with you."

She's a young girl. I was worried about that. "Paula, do you think you can handle this? It'll be ugly."

She said, "As long as I'm with you, Doc, I'll be okay."

I started grabbing things we might need, and so did she. I was a little panicked, or maybe it was more of an adrenaline rush. It's not that I wanted to go or be there, but I had to. I was afraid, and I just had to go.

The experience at that point was not too different from 9/11 when my mother was on the phone with me telling me about the Twin Towers. I thought she was exaggerating and I went outside of my office where I could see New York. I got there just in time to see the second plane hit and the building explode. Like that day, I was immediately mobilized on January 15. This is what I do. I was trained as a multiple-trauma specialist, though now I do internal medicine. Of course, not knowing the extent of the problem or the cause, many people involved were thinking back to the terrorist experience of 2001. That's just what people at the hospital, seeing this plane going down, thought. So the hospital geared for that kind of action.

In 2001, there really wasn't much help to be offered, as it sadly turned out. I did hop a ferry that day and went to the site. It wasn't running at the time, but I said to the pilot, "I have to get over there. I'm a doctor!"

He didn't hesitate. "Yes, ma'am," he said, and off we went. Five of us from my office.

The docs were stationed at St. Vincent, waiting for the injured. When I found that they weren't going to send us out, I went straight to Ground Zero, where my job became helping calm the firefighters who were going through hell, bringing out people, their own comrades, and no one alive. I was lucky to have been trained in trauma work, to get through a day like that. The scene down there was like from a disaster movie. Like the *Superman* movie when the world was destroyed. That was the picture. The whole street covered with a white film of dust, papers all over, pictures, receipts, accounts, everything covered. No doctors there, only firemen. It was a little bit dangerous, I think. And that scene was ugly. Really awful. . . .

I didn't know what I'd find as I raced to the evacuation site on January 15, but I knew what to expect. Plane crashes leave a lot of damage. There would be children, death, lots of suffering, and huge medical problems. I was second-guessing myself. "Should I have left Paula back at the office?" Then I was so very thankful that I saw about one hundred people, all alive, most in shock. They were all quiet. That amazed me. "Thank God. Thank God. They're alive," I said. I began to relax then.

The paramedics had triaged them, and I did a quick check to see if anyone was injured. I began then to work with the not-fatal but dangerous issues of hypothermia, frostbite, and shock. People were wet, and I had to get them out of their wet clothes. This presented a problem because we had no other clothes or blankets. I started out using garbage bags to wrap cold feet in! But people held on to to their clothes. It was all they had left. Even when I asked folks to get out of their shoes because hypothermia was setting in, they were reluctant. I can understand that—you cling to what you have. But clothes showed up pretty soon. I'm not sure where they came from, but it was important. People weren't always aware how close they were to hypothermia or frostbite, so I was glad to be able to get them into dry clothes. A big part of my role was to be a supportive person. Having a doctor around helps people feel like they are safe. So I was there, hopefully preventing further injury by doing some proactive work around the cold and wet issues, and being there as a voice of caring.

The only person in real danger was Barry. A paramedic asked me in a low voice to look him over. His blood pressure was low, and they couldn't get it up even with a liter of fluid. When I got to him I saw why they were so worried. He was cold, on the floor, staring, in shock, and pale. He wasn't looking good. There was black and blue in his chest wall, so I was concerned with internal injuries. But to top it off, we thought he was delusional and having hallucinations, and that's a very bad sign. He had on the captain's shirt so we kept asking him about the flight. We needed to get information and identify the captain. "Sir, are you sure you're not the captain?" we asked, and he kept saying, "I'm not the captain!" It must have driven him a bit crazy. I know passengers had been thanking him, too. He explained how he got the shirt, and then all I had to worry about was his broken sternum, his shock, hypothermia, and the possibility that his heart might have been damaged. He was the one we rushed to the hospital. I immediately followed. Thankfully, he is okay.

When Barry and Dave organized the lunch to thank the people who helped, I was so touched. I don't expect thanks. That's not why I do this work. Sometimes I get thanks—all doctors do. Sometimes I get the opposite because there are plenty of people who are angry at the physician or the situation or just life in general. But to be publicly honored, that was a wonderful feeling. It's a beautiful thing to give to a physician. When I saw Barry at the event, I felt so emotional I just wanted to hug him . . . and I did. Their giving back to us that way completed the circle. So often we do something important or life saving and then we never see the person again. It feels like the circle is left open. Knowing that Barry was trying to find me, that he remembered me—that made me very happy.

I feel like this experience—being there in a survival situation that turned out so well, being able to help, and then being thanked—has made me a softer person. My feet have landed more fully on the ground. In this profession there's disappointment every day. It's easy to become detached and caught up in the daily requirements: insurance, appointments, too much to do, people seeing physicians in some very difficult ways. Something like this is like a punch in the head. *Wake up! Remember why you do this work!* This event, the accident, and the thank-you luncheon have pulled on something deep inside me.

About a year ago, when my mother first got ill, I began to have a feeling of spirituality, something I didn't much pay attention to before that. Doctors aren't trained for that. If it's not in a book, then it's not true. This experience on the Hudson reinforced that feeling of spirituality for me. I've even taken a course in holistic medicine because I know there are things we don't know. Medicine is in its infancy, even if we sometimes think we know it all. I know that things happen for people in ways we can't understand. As doctors we are often naïve, not open to seeing the bigger picture that is beyond our control.

I've come away with two strong experiences: kind of mixed. The first is that I felt sad, here and during 9/11, that more doctors and medical personnel weren't right there on the scene. Were they not there because of fear of lawsuits? That's a sad commentary on our society, if it's true. And if the medical people aren't showing up because it's dangerous or scary, which it is, that makes me sad, too. This is our work, no matter what the price. I hope this event changes perceptions in the medical profession. I just have this impulse . . . again it comes from a long family tradition . . . of jumping into the fray to offer my services and my skills. I'm the one who says, "I was in the wrong place at the right time!" I really believe that.

But most important to me is that this eye-opening experience has become a teaching for me and one I use with patients. I had a woman in my office yesterday. She was depressed and unmotivated, and spontaneously I told her of the accident on the Hudson. "You could be dead as quickly as they almost were. Isn't it worth living? Even if it feels overwhelming?" She agreed. Living here she'd seen the whole thing, too, but for her it was an arm's length away. When I brought it closer, reminded her that this could be any of us at any time, it gave her a little motivation to go on. I told her I'd call her in three hours to see if she could take even one step in her life that felt positive. When I called her, she actually had, and she felt pretty good. I think this miracle inspired her. I know it inspired me.

I've used this teaching lesson many times since then, with patients, with people who have lost loved ones, and even with my own mother. "Why?" she asks. We never know why. That's not our job to know. A few short months after this miracle a plane and helicopter crashed in the same location, and everyone died. Why? Why do some live and others die? I think we have to live with the mystery and keep finding ways to be part of the solutions to whatever problems we face. There are so many mysteries, so much unknown. I see this in medicine, where things happen that can't be explained. This is where my spirituality helps me. I can hold these larger forces and not have to answer why. But I'll keep showing up, even though it's scary. I just have to do my part. That's who I am.

P.S. In a follow-up conversation, Hilda answers her office door to a delivery man. I hear her say, "It's not a bomb, is it?" She's attuned to danger now but is only joking, and he knows it. They laugh. Hilda tells me her mother is in the hospital, and I share that my sister is also. There are soft moments of caring about the ones we love and caring about each other's family, people we've never met. When we end, she tells me to call her if I need any help with my sister. I feel grateful to know this woman.

24
Gerry McNamara:
THE POWER OF STORY

Stories are the creative conversion of life itself into a more powerful, clearer, more meaningful experience. They are the currency of human contact.

—Robert McKee

I teach classes on writing life stories through a university continuing education program and a vibrant senior center. I love watching women and men discover the enjoyment and rewards from sifting through years or decades of memories and capturing them in their own simple voices and styles. Then I watch what happens when they share their stories with their fellow students. Eyes light up. Heads nod. The room often fills with tears, laughter, or both. Sometimes it's a dramatic story. Much more often it's a very "ordinary" story. It doesn't matter. It's the honest, authentic telling that stirs something in others. They resonate with some detail, some feeling, some image. They remember. And everyone senses the universal power of telling our stories.

The survivors of Flight 1549 have a very dramatic story to share. Most of them have felt that power of story in simply recounting what happened to them that day. People are transfixed and moved. It happens with family, friends, coworkers, church communities, teachers and students at schools, and with the media. When a survivor tells his or her story of the crash and rescue, people react. They think about miracles, about God, about gratitude, about tragedies, about fears, about death, about hope.

Soon after the crash, Gerry McNamara shared his story and learned about this power big-time. He also had to learn what to do when that power gets put in motion, especially when it's unexpected and outside the comfort zone. As you follow along, you might consider whether there might be a story of your own that may be time for you to share. Doesn't matter if it's big or small. But you might find you have a story that could benefit others in the hearing and serve you in the telling.

—Kevin

In Gerry's Words

How did all 155 of us somehow survive that crash? That was the good news that sparked all the media coverage. The story touched people of all ages, backgrounds, and beliefs. I had an unusual close-up look at this. I wrote a simple personal account of the crash of Flight 1549 and shared it with some friends and coworkers, and within weeks it went viral across the Internet and eventually landed, in its entirety, in *TIME* magazine. Sweeping across channels of communication I barely knew existed, my story must have been read by hundreds of thousands or more of people.

How did that happen? Why? What did it mean to me not only to have been granted this second chance at life but to suddenly find myself at the center of part of the public response? Even now I don't have all the answers, but I have unearthed some clues.

First, I need to make clear that I was never seeking the attention or notoriety. Outside of my responsibilities as a Managing Partner with Heidrick & Struggles in New York, I tend to be a private person. I didn't even know about *TIME* getting hold of my account until someone sent me the online version. I wrote about my experience on Flight 1549 first as a journaling exercise for myself, my wife, Debbie, and my three college-age children. I wanted to record the most important details:

- How I had been scheduled on a later flight that day, and how, when I moved up to Flight 1549 out of LaGuardia, I had this fleeting thought: *Did I just place myself on a flight I should not be on?*
- Seeing the pilot as I boarded and thinking: I like to see gray hair in the cockpit!
- Hearing that pilot's command to "Brace for impact" and remembering that very same command spoken on a helicopter while serving as a Marine officer.
- Looking out the window and seeing that dark green water that I knew would be freezing, then remembering how I had swum in those same Hudson waters as a boy.
- Standing on the wing when a woman slipped off, and

with the help of a fellow passenger, pulling her back up and advising her to kneel on the wing to keep from slipping off again.

■ Noting that the tide was moving out because we were tracking slowly south toward Ellis Island, the Statue of Liberty, and the Battery.

■ Grabbing a man unable to move his legs to climb the Jacob's ladder and hoisting him up into the ferry.

I added four simple life lessons I had scribbled on a card, a mix of personal and practical:

1. Cherish your families as never before, and go to great lengths to keep your promises.
2. Be thankful and grateful for everything you have, and don't worry about the things you don't have.
3. Keep in shape. You never know when you'll be called upon to save your own life or help someone else save theirs.
4. When you fly, wear practical clothing. You never know when you'll end up in an emergency or on an icy wing in flip-flops and pajamas and are of absolutely no use to yourself or anyone else.

Shortly afterward I was contacted by the guardian of our company newsletter. "Since so many of our employees fly regularly, I know they'd appreciate reading about this incredible event you experienced. Would you write something for our newsletter?" she asked.

I thought about this for a moment. "Well, I did write something for my family, but I did not mean for so many people to see it," I said. "But if you think it can be helpful to others, you can put that in the newsletter. It would be a great way for me to communicate thanks to all those across the firm who have sent expressions of support and relief for my survival."

That's how it started. Initially it circulated to our 1,700 employees. From there, I don't know exactly when or how it reached the tipping point. As best I can tell, someone from our firm decided to send it to a colleague at a competing firm; the person who received it there sent it to someone at another company; new recipients passed it on to others they knew; and suddenly my simple account was being posted on forums and entities all over the world. I couldn't decide what was more amazing: how quickly it spread, or the responses that filled my voice mail and in-box. A few of the many examples:

- A fellow military officer offering his "Bravo Zulu for a job well done" and a former Marine offering his reflections at surviving an ambush more than forty years earlier.
- A former test pilot resonating with my description of what normally would happen on a water landing like ours.
- A school guidance counselor explaining how he had passed my story along to his own children to learn from it.
- A woman sharing her heartfelt account of surviving her own very different life-threatening accident.

A frequent traveler acknowledging that he also would often have those fleeting doubts about the rightness of making a last-minute schedule change. Even more striking was the e-mail from a colleague who recalled my voice mail message the morning of the flight. "I hope to head home safely to Charlotte this afternoon," I had said, "God willing."

I also received letters, including one with a California lottery ticket stuck inside the envelope. Coincidentally, one e-mail respondent advised that I didn't need to ever play the lottery because I had already won!

Each time I would leave for a business trip, dozens of new responses would be waiting for me upon my return. I was touched by words like "The world is better off with you and all of those passengers surviving." I was moved by the woman thanking me for honoring Marines, because her late husband had earned five purple hearts. Many others resonated with my observation about how comforting it was to see a gray-haired man in the cockpit. And I was especially surprised at how many people commented on my four simple life lessons.

While I deeply appreciated this completely unexpected response, I have to be honest. At first I regarded it all as a bit of a distraction. When you travel extensively for your job and commute from a New York office to a home in Charlotte, your schedule doesn't leave much room to pore through hundreds of nonwork e-mails.

But as the deluge continued, I thought more about what was happening. This really wasn't about me. The miracle itself had stirred people, and something about my simple way of personalizing it had left a mark. People, many I didn't even know, were taking time from their own busy lives to reach out to me and share something meaningful about themselves. How could that be a nuisance? Maybe we were all trying to figure out what God was trying to achieve through this miracle. I certainly don't know—maybe someone on our plane will find the cure for cancer or go on to some other achievement that can make a major difference in our world. Finally, it hit me: *You're supposed to tell this story. You've started something and it's reaching people. Yes, it can be a distraction at times, but this is a way to recognize and honor the gift that you received. You need to keep doing this!*

So let the trail go far and wide, I decided. I even opened myself to speaking in public about my story and what I believe we all can learn from it. Yes, I'm still a private person, but I'm fifty-five years old and have lived through having my head shaved at Quantico and now a plane crash in the Hudson. How daunting can it be to stand in front of a live audience and talk about my life? I started out at Gardner-Webb University, where my son John was a student, and then spoke to a leadership group and a men's Bible group. I'm still not looking for attention, just keeping an eye out for where I might help.

Sharing about my life has rekindled some poignant memories. Take that reference in my story to swimming in the

Hudson River. I grew up in Rockaway Beach, the little seaside community in Queens that was hit hard when many fire-fighters, police officers, and businessmen and -women who lived there perished on 9/11 and then again two months later when American Airlines Flight 587 out of JFK Airport crashed there. My dad, a fire officer who had served in the Coast Guard during World War II, and mom somehow found the resources to send my five siblings and me to private school. I ran cross-country and track at LaSalle Academy, which didn't have a track of its own. Sometimes we ran along the East River or to Central Park, and during warm spring days we would detour down to the Hudson, climb over the fences at the piers, and plunge in.

We'd swim for ten or fourteen minutes until a worker would yell, "You kids get out of there! Don't you know there are all kinds of things in that water you could impale your-self on?" No doubt he was referring to rusted washing machines and dryers, maybe even parts of a sunken ship. We'd just laugh, run back to school, and tell our coach, "We had a great workout!" Years later, friends who heard of my exploits and knew just how filthy the Hudson was back then would say, "Gerry, you're lucky you don't have three ears." When I was rescued from the river on January 15, I noted how the Hudson is a lot cleaner these days, though it sure was a lot colder.

My "brace for impact" echo stemmed from a helicopter incident during a North Atlantic Marine training exercise. The helicopter fell twenty feet, but on that day, as on Flight

1549, no one was seriously hurt. My Marine background shaped my preparations before the US Airways crash. As we descended I realized we had a couple of minutes of flight remaining and focused on prayer, thanking God for the gift of his Son and asking him to care for my wife and children. I prayed for courage and the strength to act with honor. If we somehow survived and were fighting for our lives in a submerged plane, like those images of the Titanic, all I asked was that I would behave courageously and try to help others.

I've done my best to adhere to those life lessons I wrote about, beginning with "Cherish your family as never before." My kids, John, Greg, and Meghan, were all in college when Flight 1549 landed in the Hudson, and in those emotional days afterward, I found myself thinking: they need me now more than ever. So in March, just two months after the crash, Debbie and I steered all our schedules to get the whole family together for a vacation in Florence, Italy, where my daughter was on a study-abroad program. We had a wonderful time: eating real Italian food, drinking fantastic wine, and seeing the centuries-old historic sites that remind us how young our country really is. It was my first vacation in three years! During one moment I took in the contrast: what could have been versus the scene of us all together enjoying everything life has to offer. Debbie and I even went back in April for Meghan's twenty-first birthday, taking her on a train excursion to Sorrento.

When I speak in public, I also emphasize my life lesson about being grateful for what we have and not worrying about the things we don't have. It saddens me to see the materialism and consumerism that drives so much of our society these days. When Flight 1549 went down in the Hudson, what spurred us all on was simply this: to survive, to celebrate life. Could there be a message there for us all?

25
Claudette Mason:
NEW MIRACLES

Now faith is the substance of things hoped for, the evidence of things not seen.

—Hebrews 11:1

As she celebrated coming home alive from the crash, Claudette could count her many blessings. A loving husband. A daughter making her way in the world as an adult. A big, close family back home in Virginia. An exciting job she has worked hard to step into and excel at. A lively Memphis church that lifts her spirits. She sings her praises for all of that and for being spared on the Hudson, and she looks for ways to give back. "I've always been a person who likes to give to others," she says. "Once I was Christmas shopping in a mall, and a woman commented on how much she liked the broach I was wearing. A few minutes later I ran out of the store, chased her down, and gave her my broach. Now I feel I have more to give to my family and to my community. I like that feeling."

Yet sometimes Claudette cries. And sometimes she feels yearnings. Just like we all do. Her yearnings aren't about money or possessions. She grew up on the other side of the *tracks and laughs about how twenty-eight family members recently piled into her house and slept on air mattresses so they could enjoy a Fourth of July celebration together. When we talk, I don't know what all of Claudette's yearnings might be. I would imagine they are about love, about unity, about health, about God and the wonders of spirit. During our interview she reveals one of those yearnings to me and the surprising twist that emerged related to it as a result of the crash. It's a new miracle. Isn't it amazing how that can happen? Something really, really good happens in our lives (though probably not on the level of surviving a plane crash!), and then, quite unexpectedly, something else comes along that also makes us smile, laugh, sing praises. We see the connection. And we wonder: do miracles really breed new miracles?*

—Kevin

In Claudette's Words

"THE FAMILY THAT PRAYS TOGETHER stays together." It may be a common saying, but it really defined life growing up in Franklin, Virginia, a tiny city not far from Norfolk. My parents, my nine older siblings, and I were mainstays at the First Baptist Church Hall Street in Franklin all through my childhood. After I went off to college in the big city of Richmond, I came back to Franklin and served the church in multiple roles: youth leader, women's ministry, choir member, chairman of the finance board. Today I live outside Memphis, where I'm a member of the Oak Grove Missionary Baptist Church. It's a much bigger church, and I'm not as involved as a volunteer, but the importance of family praying together has never been more important to me. It took the crash of Flight 1549 on the Hudson River to remind me just how important.

When our plane was going down that day, I, like many passengers, reached for my cell phone. I was going to die, and I had to reach out to my family, to feel that connection one final time. But the lines were jammed. When I closed my eyes I actually found myself with these fleeting thoughts: *Well, my double indemnity will kick in and US Airways will step up. They'll take care of my family. They'll be okay.* . . . Then I just saw their warm faces and felt our love, and I locked arms with the man sitting next to me and prayed a prayer of thanksgiving.

Minutes later, standing on the water on the wing before any rescue ferry had closed in, I had a second chance! I gripped my cell in my freezing fingers and tried my husband Alfred. No luck there, but when I called my daughter, Lynette, I reached her at a clothing store. I tried to explain about the crash but she was so emotional that she could hardly listen. The kindly woman working there picked up the phone and offered to help. My daughter told her I desperately wanted to reach my husband, and she immediately plugged Alfred in on a conference call. Within seconds I was talking to both my husband and my daughter.

"My plane crashed," I said again, as calmly as I could. "I'm standing on the wing of the plane in the water right now. I don't know what's going to happen . . . if I'll make it . . . so I just want you to know that I love you. No matter what happens, I love you."

With that, I took a deep breath and focused on keeping my balance on the slippery wing. I had said what I needed to say. I knew that through Alfred and Lynette, my message would be passed on to my six brothers and three sisters, to my twenty-eight nieces and nephews, to my three brothers-in-law and five sisters-in-law, and to Mom with her Alzheimer's and Dad with his breathing problems back in Franklin. They would all know that I had sent my love to them. That's all I could do.

There wasn't much time for memories. Those rescue ferries soon converged, we were whisked to the pier, and it became clear that we had been saved by the hand of God. But those memories were deeply embedded in my heart, and had we been floating out there much longer, uncertain of our fate, many of them would have come tumbling out.

Like how I got my nickname, Ducky. Dad started calling me that because I loved frolicking in water. Outside I'd play in any puddle or pond, and inside you could always find me splashing around in the tub and, as I have been reminded too many times, even in the toilet. He still calls me Ducky. So do most of my family.

I might have flashed back to going door-to-door collecting signatures for petitions to help my father in his battle against the giants when I was eight. This man with a seventh-grade education had built up a successful local transportation business, and he had it in his mind that he could expand beyond the state of Virginia and run charter bus services nationally. Of course, a couple of big name entities had that market pretty well cornered. While I didn't understand all the legal issues, I didn't hesitate to help. I'd sit down at a typewriter and peck away with one finger to draft letters to the US Commerce Department or some other officious-sounding place. This business was part of all our lives. I felt proud when he would come home after midnight, and we would clean out his bus for the next day's charter. He poured hours and hours into this legal struggle over months, but he never gave up, and he won. At one point the Franklin Bus Service had fourteen charter busses.

"Ducky," he would say, "if you really want something, you have to work for it."

I remember the first time I walked onto one of our busses and heard the driver talking on a CB radio. "How is that possible?" I asked. As soon as I was old enough to get my license, it was my turn to help out with the driving. I would get up before 5 AM and get behind the wheel of the most basic vehicle in our fleet: a Ford Country Squire station wagon with the wood grain panels. I might transport four or five kidney patients going in for their morning dialysis treatments before heading home to get ready for school. After school I'd drive back to Norfolk to pick up the patients from the after-lunch run.

Over time, I was entrusted with driving the vans with the higher passenger capacity. I know Dad was proud, but mostly what I remember was his teasing. You see, he was an avid hunter, but he had never shot a deer. When I was driving in those predawn hours, I seemed to have a knack for hitting deer on the road. "Ducky, you got another deer?" he would say. "I guess you're the hunter around here." I would just laugh.

After college, I returned to Franklin but went to work for the big local paper manufacturer. My husband, Alfred, worked there, too, and we might have stayed in my hometown had not International Paper bought the company in 1999. IP's global headquarters is based in Memphis, and although it was painful to separate from my family, I recognized that moving was right for my future.

So I left home, and from my roots starting out as a simple customer service rep, I now hold major responsibility as a sales rep who travels far and wide. Like Dad said, if you really want something you have to work for it. Even from Memphis, I maintain an active role in important family matters. Though the youngest of ten children, I am often looked up to as a key decision maker on matters related to my parents. I call home every day and come back for frequent visits. I have had to adjust, as so many of us do, to my mother sometimes recognizing me and sometimes not. It's difficult. . . . Recently, both my parents were in the hospital at the same time as my mother-in-law, who passed away just a few months after the Hudson.

Since the crash, I have felt that I can't miss a beat with them. My family needs me, relies on me, confides in me. They feel that security of having me here to help them now, after enduring those moments of worrying about me just after the crash. I still cry sometimes about what almost happened that day. I call them my "silent cries." At work I may carefully close my door, cry for a few moments, then open the door and get on with my day. Other times in bed late at night I may cry, and not even Alfred will know.

Often the crying doesn't feel like sadness. It's more just tears at how awesome what God did was. He kept me here not only for my family but also to witness the inauguration of Barack Obama, a moment that as an African American woman filled me with pride. Lord, if I had not been able to see that day!

I also need to keep being there for my family because after the crash they were there for me. I still shake my head when I remember the plan: my oldest brother, Gurnie Junior, whom we call Bubba, had driven up to New York and was going to drive me as far as Laurel, Maryland. From there, my brother Ricky would take me to Franklin to see family. After that reunion, my brother Larry would drive me to Greensboro, North Carolina, where my brother Bobby, whose real name is Claude, would be waiting to shuttle me to Newport, Tennessee. Alfred would handle the last leg to Memphis.

"How did you think this up so quickly?" I asked. Only in a family that grew up in a transportation business could a plan like this be cooked up at all. Still, I had to decline this family shuttle service. For one thing, it was snowing in the Northeast and the last thing I needed was to have anyone get killed or injured in a car accident while trying to rescue me. Second, I knew that if I went right to Virginia, they would never let me go! More important, though my family was right to assume I really did not want to fly, I was determined to conquer that fear right away. I'm a sales rep—traveling is what I do.

On the flight home, I tried to imagine Dad watching me on CNN getting on that rescue boat. I thought again of the passing of years, the changing of the times, and what has endured. Not long before the crash I was with Dad when he stepped onto one of those modern busses with the GPS navigation system, and he blurted out, "How in the world is that possible?" Just like me trying to make sense of CB radio.

When I got home, my husband, Alfred, and I understood that we now shared a new bond. Two and a half years earlier, he had his own brush with death, collapsing at work with a stroke. When I rushed over to see him, I rubbed under his chin and said, "It's going to be okay. It's going to be okay." Now he was reassuring me, even coming with me to church on Sunday, something he usually only did on special occasions. My husband has faith in his own way but had not committed to any church since he was a boy. He was curious about my church and would listen when I would sometimes retell the sermon on Sundays, but he held the line. Given my beliefs about family and prayer, I have to admit this did trouble me. Do you ever feel that way about a loved one? Alfred has always been everything a husband should be, but this one thing was missing. How I wished it wasn't.

At the service that Sunday after the crash, Reverend Donald Johnson told the congregation that I had been on the

Miracle on the Hudson plane. The shouting and praising shot up to the rafters! Then, even before the pastor could make his regular invitation that began "I open the doors to the church," my husband bolted up from his seat and surged toward the front of the church. I scampered to follow and was right there sitting beside him when my husband, at last, became a member of my church.

"It was when you called from the plane that day," he whispered. "When I was driving home I just kept saying, 'Lord, if you return her to me safely I'll join her church. Bring her home and I'll join her church.'"

We have gone over that story many times since that day. And now he sits with me in my church, *our* church, on a regular basis. I don't have to come home and recreate the sermon; we hear it together. Sometimes it goes in so direct, we just sit there holding hands and cry. Even Lynette, who has come back to Memphis after living in DC, has joined the church. The family that prays together stays together. I don't know what your religious beliefs may be, or how this may sound to you, but it is the truth: if I had to do that crash and rescue all over again for my husband to join my church, I would.

26
Jerry Shanko:
DREAMING OF TOMORROW

Oh no, not Jerry—he's going to have a baby!

—Coworker of Jerry Shanko reacting
to early reports of the Hudson River crash

I've been trying for weeks to pin down an interview time with Jerry, and it's not working out. Though I know he wants to participate in our book, he hasn't been returning my phone or e-mail messages. If I did not know his story from a much earlier interview, I might be concerned that something is wrong. But I do know, and I am not worried. Jerry and his wife have been expecting the birth of their first child. When he finally responds, with many apologies for not getting back to me sooner, he eagerly fills me in on the details of the big moment and the glorious time since then.

I'm a first-time father myself, and I appreciate the chance to relive my own memories as he shares his. There's a special poignancy about this birth. Jerry's wife was pregnant when the plane crashed. We all know what that means, could have meant. But instead of the almost unspeakable tragedy for Jerry, his wife, and unborn child, they have all entered together that time not only of joy but of mystery.

What will our child become? It's something we all wonder from those first moments of watching our child sleep, or grasp a finger, or just stare at the ceiling. And when I invite Jerry to ponder that mystery of his child's future, I can tell that this is no fanciful exercise for him. When he's finished sharing his thoughts about this, which you will read about in his story, I strongly suspect he's going to be thinking about it some more. He has stepped into a rare mystery: moving from the brink of death to observing and reveling in a new life. This is real in a physical sense for Jerry, but it's also true in the broader sense for any of us who have come back from something or somewhere trying or traumatic. If we look with eyes of wonder and mystery, we may find new life right before us.

—Kevin

In Jerry's Words

"I WOULD LOVE TO MEET the pilot and shake his hand and thank him that I still have the chance to see my baby." Those were my words, as they appeared at the end of an article in *People* magazine a few weeks after Captain Sullenberger glided Flight 1549 down to a safe landing in the Hudson River. I did get to meet and thank him during the reunion of Sully and the passengers in Charlotte as part of the *60 Minutes* filming in February. My wife, Rebecca, five months pregnant when it all happened, was there, too. I have a photo of her shaking hands with Sully. You can see a tear in Rebecca's eye. That photo is priceless.

Now, the next time I see that pilot or any other fellow survivors of Flight 1549, I'll no doubt be holding Samantha Austin Shanko, born May 29, 2009, weighing in at eight pounds, eleven ounces, and twenty-one inches long—pretty amazing for a small wife. I didn't have to wait long to see my baby when she was born because I was right there. Boy, was I there! I had attended all the prebirth classes and was ready to play a role, but to be honest, I believed that once the curtain went up, I would mostly be a bystander. But there I was in that delivery room with just the doctor, one nurse, Rebecca, and me. I never left my wife's side the entire time. Fortunately, with induced labor, that was just a 9 a.m. to 4:31 p.m. workday. My job was to offer words of encouragement: "It's okay, honey, you're doing fine. Keep it up. Everything's going great."

And it was great, especially when I held up my baby and immediately got choked up. We didn't know the gender ahead of time, and though everyone around us kept insisting it would be a boy, I just knew somehow it would be a girl. This was my first child, the moment I had been somehow spared to live for. Spared by Sully's amazing landing. Spared by all those other factors that had to fit perfectly together and did. The calm winds. The snow that had fallen that morning but had stopped by afternoon. The timing . . . I remember one of the first responders telling me, "This happened during our shift change. You were really lucky. If it had been five minutes later, who knows?" The next day I looked out at the Hudson and noticed ice chunks thirty feet from shore. What if that ice had surrounded the wings of our plane when we tried to balance ourselves on them? It was as if at every possible point where something could have gone wrong, God said, "I'll take care of that."

Samantha arrived not only as our firstborn but the first grandchild in both our families. I'm thirty-one, and my younger sister Heidi and Rebecca's younger brother Clark do not have families yet, so you know this was a big event. Rebecca's parents and brother came up from Greenville for the birth, and her mother stayed with us for the first five days we were home, and soon after they left, my parents came down from Pittsburgh for five days. Now it's time for the road trips, first to Greenville to see the rest of Rebecca's family, and then we'll see how Samantha does in a car for eight hours to Pittsburgh for my family. Everyone says Samantha looks like me, but I can't see it. She looks too good for that to be true! She's also extremely quiet—we usually have to wake her up to feed her. Just the perfect first baby. I've been on family leave, soaking up every minute of it.

You need to understand, even before the crash I never expected to be a father. Not that long ago I was well into my twenties and wondering if I was destined to stay single. No kids. No grandkids for my mom and dad. Maybe other people start families much later in life, but I couldn't see that far ahead. Then Rebecca came along. We had actually known each other a bit from church, but now something just seemed to click. She's a really solid person, she has a fun personality, and she knew I needed another goofball. I have a wicked sense of humor sometimes. It even came out around the birth: when Samantha was several days overdue I quipped, "See, she's already lazy and stubborn and she hasn't even entered the world yet." Rebecca laughed with me. We dated awhile, got engaged, and by the time we married we were both very clear that we wanted children. I just didn't think it would happen so fast. Before I knew it, I was coming home from work one day, and Rebecca was smiling, and I said, "Oh yeah, we're having a baby!"

We hadn't gotten around to preparing a nursery by late 2008. "We'll get to it soon after the holidays," we kept saying. But then January 15 came along, and for a while there, the whole plan, our whole future as a new family, got tossed up in the air. In those final seconds in the cabin, I noticed a few other passengers reaching for their cell phones. I could hear them saying things like "I just wanted you to know I love you." There was no way I was going to leave a message like that for Rebecca. It would have been traumatizing for her, and if she suddenly got all shook up from hearing words like that, what would that do to the baby?

So I focused on exactly what was happening in front of me. When I finally accepted that we were landing on water, all I had in my mind were those images from Hollywood of planes breaking apart upon crashing into the ocean. I was sure that would happen to us. I wonder today about those passengers on the Air France crash. If their plane were still intact as it plummeted toward the Atlantic Ocean, did any of them carry images of *our* plane making its amazing and safe landing? Did they think maybe they were going to make it, too? It gives me shivers to think about.

After we landed on the Hudson, I wound up on one of the wings, so impressed, as we all were, by everyone's willingness to reach out to help the next person. I had brought out two seat cushions, and after one of the guys handed me a life jacket, I went back into the cabin with him to get more. We grabbed as many as we could with both hands and tossed them out to other passengers trying to hold those vulnerable positions on the icy, slippery wings. "Toss out some more!" they shouted. And we did. The rescue ferries seemed to be a lot longer coming to our side. When I was convinced that we were all going to make it, I called Rebecca.

We didn't get to fixing the nursery for quite a while. Actually, it was just a few weeks before the due date when we added the finishing touches. My wife and I just appreciated our time, so grateful that we were still together as we waited for our lives to change in such a joyful way. Of course, I can't say that I spent every waking nonwork moment rubbing Rebecca's belly and going to baby classes. I did take time out to root the Steelers on to the Super Bowl championship. I grew up in Pittsburgh, and I've always been a big sports fan. My dad, who did shift work much of his life, had been on the waiting list for Steelers season tickets for ten years before he finally was selected. I've had plenty of thrills with my home team over the years and collected my share of autographs and memorabilia. It was great to be champions again.

Then, in the spring I got to watch the Pittsburgh Penguins in their run through the playoffs. The Stanley Cup finals between the Penguins and Detroit Red Wings began the night after Samantha was born. Did I watch? Yep, the whole game. I watched the entire glorious series while Rebecca kept saying, "I will be so glad when this is over." It finished with the Penguins hoisting the Stanley Cup. I began joking to friends, "What an unbelievable six months: surviving a plane crash, Samantha's birth, and the Steelers and Penguins both winning the championship! I think I should start playing the lottery." But five years from now if you ask me which '09 event was the most important, I know I will not hesitate to answer: Samantha.

I don't know how or when I might tell her about the Hudson River crash as she gets older. I will keep one of those dramatic photos of us standing on the wings, and I recently received one of those copies of the illustration with those hands holding up the plane in the water. I'll probably show her those. Whatever I say about it, I'm sure it will be joyous. I have heard how some of the other passengers have been considering lawsuits as a way to be further compensated for the experience. I can't understand that. To me, we were just so, so blessed. We had the happy ending, not like my own family back home a few years ago when my cousin Steven was shot down in his helicopter in Afghanistan while on a rescue mission in support of Special Ops Forces. Only one member of the ground force survived. It was the same operation in which Michael T. Murphy perished [which Scott Koen talks about in his story]. But in our potential tragedy on the Hudson, we all lived. We don't need more settlements.

I remember what Sully's wife said in their *60 Minutes* interview when reading a letter someone wrote about how, when a life is saved, you never know what that person is going to do. It's so true. I don't know what the future will hold for me, for any of us, in the next five years or ten years. I don't think the impact of all this is done. I had not really talked to anyone in any counseling or therapy after the crash. There was so much more going on then, but I plan to seek some counseling now. The crash is not my identity, and I don't feel a need to talk about it all the time, but it is important. I know it's affected me. And I know it's affected *her.* If the crash had all turned out differently, my wife probably would have wound up living with her family in Greenville. That's the life Samantha would have known. A ton of love and support, but different. Now, I am a part of that life, and who knows what her future has in store? It's amazing just to stop and think about it.

I have an image. I'm walking her down the aisle on her wedding day. I will be filled with joy and happiness, and maybe some sadness at the passage. But I'll also remember back to January 15, 2009. And I'll shed another tear.

REFLECTIONS

> *Happiness is not so much in having as sharing.*
>
> —Norman MacEwan

Life is always about giving and receiving. Each breath we take pulls in oxygen from our whole world and each out breath returns it. In our interconnectedness we always share. We share the air, the planet, its resources, the pie on the table. Sometimes we share the best of who we are, sometimes . . . well, we know that what we sometimes give back to our world is not our best! And in sharing, we know ourselves in relationship. We may give someone that last piece of pie, or they may give it to us. And gratitude comes not only in being given to, but in giving. *What do we have to be grateful for?* There is so much, even when times are hard. Expressing that gratitude and, even more basically, expressing the truth of ourselves completes a circle. The gift given must be received. The thank-you offered must be heard. Both the giver and the receiver are complete.

As we face crises or even the normal challenges of everyday life, we are bound to grow and change. Beth, for instance, grew from a person who was just okay with her life to a person who touched, felt, breathed, talked, and hugged life. Beth is being herself, without reservations, as she continues her quest for meaningful contact through her hugs. She is sharing herself. But for many of us, expressing ourselves in the forms of hugs or public speaking or anything in between is not easy. We carry the fear that it is not okay to fully express

ourselves or even to be ourselves. In the face of a strong pull
to cling to safety, to hold on, to hide, to stay comfortable, we
may hold back that most essential aspect of who we all are:
our ability to share, free of fear.

What if I just shared what was true for me? As we ask that question, a whole world of possibilities opens up. And for each of
us who chooses to move in that direction, even a little bit, our
lives will be "more." The sunshine will be brighter. The good
work we've done, be it cleaning the house or performing surgery, will be felt as important work. Our appreciation for
others will be deeper. Our valuing of ourselves will be truer.
Our ability to forgive will come more easily. And all of this
because we opened our hearts and minds, in big or little ways,
and shared ourselves with the world.

Speaking from the heart is something all of us do, sometimes. Each way will be unique. Dave's version is speaking to
hundreds of people; Gerry's is quietly telling his story to colleagues; Claudette's is sharing her faith. What would it be like
to open the door to speaking from the heart more fully and
more often? We don't need an audience to let our hearts lead
the way. A smile, a touch, a generous act, and a kind word to
one person or many are all ways of "speaking" from the heart.
Dave is right that something happens when we reach out to
another with an open heart. Something happens for them,
and something happens for us. Trained as we are to be strong,
to keep it together, to not look weak, many of us have lost
our tears ... and sometimes our laughter. And when we share,
deeply, we touch both.

It doesn't take a great deal of insight to realize the world would be a better place if we all spoke from the heart, tears or not. If we all lived from the heart in our little and our big actions, we too would be changing the world, one moment to the next, in each act of kindness, in every word. Every tear would tell a truth. Every laugh would carry our joy. Every hug would express our love.

Sharing opens doors. Our passengers keep experiencing this over and over again. They've shared their story, and it has resonated with a world of people. More than one of our passengers has encountered a World War II veteran, and those long-ago soldiers were touched and moved by this twenty-first century miracle story, for they too could feel their own very old story of near death and a new life. And, of course, these stories have touched so many others. The story is powerful, and the storytellers are even more so. The impact continues, even in ways no one will ever know.

Part V
A Miracle to Build On

How wonderful it is that nobody need wait a single moment before starting to improve the world.

—Anne Frank

27

RIPPLES

Ripple Effect (n): The effect of one event setting off other events in an unexpected way.

—Wiktionary

ON THE AFTERNOON OF January 15, 2009, Rex Babin, like millions of us all over the country and the world, sat entranced by those TV images of the plane floating down the Hudson as passengers held their ground on the water-covered wings. As a political cartoonist for the *Sacramento Bee*, in the seat of state government in California, his work stems mostly from political issues. But he immediately recognized the Miracle on the Hudson as "the Talker," an event that sparks everyone's interest. He had to draw it.

But how did Rex really feel about those images? What did he most want to capture? He gave the matter a great deal of thought. That's when the idea of depicting two large, loving hands holding up the wings of Flight 1549 and the passengers standing so calmly on them in the Hudson River began to take shape.

Rex studied his own hands. He even took the rare step, for him, of looking at a resource book on drawing hands.

"I wanted to get those hands just right," he says.

The finished work appeared in the Sunday, January 18, 2009, edition of the *Sacramento Bee*. Within days, his cartoon had swept across the Internet. Like the miracle itself, Rex Babin had touched those who saw his image of it, especially those with strong religious beliefs.

"You could say it was divine inspiration," he says. "I'm a person of faith. I do believe there is a Higher Power. Generally that's something I keep to myself. But my gut feeling about this was that whatever your belief, there was *something* going on there that day. It could mean there is a God. It could just mean there was a lot of luck, or it was the work of the crew, or a combination of all these things. Or maybe it really means that everyone on that plane just did not have their expiration date punched that day. So I went outside my comfort zone."

Isn't that what anything we may call a miracle does: take us outside our comfort zones? Miracles stir us to reflect, to wonder, to feel, to search. We may find ourselves making sense of the world around us in a very different or stronger light. On January 15 many of us were trying to capture what this stunning crash landing and survival was all about, and what it meant. Where we might have been doing it through words, or prayer, Rex Babin was doing it through art. For many, the messages were primarily about God, religion, or spirituality. For others, the answers might have taken a different but no less meaningful form. For some, the word *miracle* itself might not have even fit. Rex noticed this wide-ranging experience in the varied conclusions people drew upon studying his illustration.

"The way I see it, it's open to interpretation," he explains. "Many people see it as Sully's hands holding the plane. Others see it as female hands. But many people seem to respond to the tender way the hands are holding the wings, not grabbing it. They can see the magic."

As you might imagine, the survivors of Flight 1549 had an immediate and profound response to this rendering of the moment forever etched in their souls. Dozens personally reached out to Rex, expressing their appreciation, gratitude, caring. "So many sweet words on beautiful thank-you cards," he beams. "I even had people ask me if they could use the image to make quilts. Well, of course they can. Somewhere there are quilts being stitched of my cartoon. It's amazing."

It took him a while to get used to the positive outpouring. As a political cartoonist charged with illustrating pointed views in an evocative way, he understands that the feelings of those with opposing views get evoked, too. He was used to the abuse. He wasn't so used to the love.

"I'm glad it has buoyed the passengers, and, yeah, it's buoyed me, too," he acknowledges. "It's been neat to share this connection that comes through faith. I just sensed that the image of what we all saw in the Hudson was something people were going to feel good about, so now they had something to help them revel in, to celebrate it."

With the reveling has come a steady and rising stream of requests from the passengers and their loved ones: was it possible for Rex to send them copies of his illustration so they and their families could display them in their homes? Sure, it was possible. Usually there would be a basic service fee, but not for survivors of Flight 1549. Rex was soon cranking out scores of personal copies, complete with passenger name and seat number.

"I would tell them, 'I'm just sending it to you because you as a passenger contributed to my day,'" relates Rex. "I'm grateful to be able to do what I do professionally, to view these major events and express them for others to see. This was a way to give that gratitude back."

The connections forged between Rex and the passengers of Flight 1549 illustrate how an event like the Hudson River miracle influences others in ever widening circles. A group of people walk away from an experience they expected would end their lives. Someone sees it and captures it, stirring countless others to deepen their own authentic response. The passengers reach out to the cartoonist with gratitude and caring, and the cartoonist extends the appreciation back to them. And so it grows. Ripples extending across the river.

The Circle of Life

The impact of this miracle on the lives of those most directly involved is clear. The passengers, having touched a deeper sense of purpose, have gone back into their worlds to share their truth—in speeches, in stories, in private wishes, and dreams shared with their loved ones. They share it in good deeds and in self-care. The doors to the sinking plane opened onto the Hudson River, onto life rafts and incoming rescue boats. The doors to a new life opened in the days and weeks and months that followed. Some doors that opened were big, some small. Wishes became realities. Inner knowing became words shared out loud. Feelings, once hidden, were allowed to be visible. Faith discovered or enriched was transformed into good works. This is the circle of life. . . .

Warren's great-grandfather recites a Bible verse on his deathbed, and forty years later Warren's son memorizes it to help him cope with a car accident. Deep in the middle of interviewing passengers, Dorothy hears Warren's words and repeats them to her sister, at death's door in an ICU. Her sister responds, a slight smile, the beginning of a recovery. Where else will this ripple take us?

Lt. Michael Murphy dies, trying valiantly to save his men in combat in Afghanistan, and years later a boat carrying his name, steered by Scott Koen, pulls people from the wreckage of Flight 1549. Lt. Murphy's father learns of what happens and is touched to see his son's legacy carried on.

Upon coming home from the Hudson, the passengers of Flight 1549 were embraced by family, friends, and strangers at every turn. They were honored in their churches, cheered in their workplaces, courted by the media, and engulfed with well wishes from people they hadn't seen in years, or decades. Why? They were symbols of a miracle, carriers of hope, reminders that bad things do sometimes turn out right. People wanted to share in that spirit, to touch it.

And just as the miracle has lived on for our travelers and those around them, so too can it continue for all of *us*. Whether we felt the hands of God involved and resonate with that image from Rex Babin, or we simply marveled at the work of Sully Sullenberger and everyone else at the scene, we can come back again and again to those images of people on the wings of a sinking plane and apply them to our lives. We can touch the ripples. If, that is, we choose to. If we keep paying attention.

Motivational speaker Jim Rohn sums up the real-life work of miracles this way: "I have found in life that if you want a miracle you first need to do whatever it is you can do—if that's to plant, then plant; if it is to read, then read; if it is to change, then change; if it is to study, then study; if it is to work, then work; whatever you have to do. And then you will be well on your way of doing the labor that works miracles."

Clearly, Sully knew this already. He worked hard for years to execute a "miracle" landing, though he has shied away from that term himself. Our passengers, our first responders, families and friends, we the authors, and you the reader are all poised, ready to do the work that allows a miracle to happen. The ripples beckon us to be the person we want to be, the person we truly and deeply are.

Each of us must choose where the ripples from Flight 1549 may take us. We may walk away with:

- A deeper respect for our heroes
- A stronger sense of life purpose
- Gratitude
- A call to community
- A new appreciation for family and loved ones
- Love
- A sense of peace
- An acceptance of life
- Wisdom
- A renewed connection to spirit
- Faith
- An awareness of something new emerging
- Healing
- An interest in quiet time and slowing down
- A curiosity about ourselves and our feelings
- An inclination to reach out to others
- A commitment to personal and global change
- Transformation

The ripples also may leave us with another, perhaps even more important discovery. Miracles really are not limited to a plane crash in which everyone goes home alive. They can emerge on any given day, in the midst of any routine of life. Someone does something unexpected, and it touches us. We read or hear a message, and it reminds us of possibilities. We witness an act that blends wisdom with caring and compassion, and we are inspired to summon more of those qualities in ourselves. Even in a crisis, in any moment of fear or sadness, a glimmer of light can remind us of the larger world. And then the new miracles begin.

Our future is a mystery, but the lessons we learn with the help from our travelers can help guide us. Like our passengers and first responders, we are invited to see each day as a new beginning. All of us can wake up tomorrow and see that new day, if we choose to. And if tomorrow is a new day, it will be full of surprises, full of possibilities, full of life.

28
GOING FORWARD

*There are many ways of going forward, but only
one way of standing still.*

—Franklin D. Roosevelt

FROM THAT FIRST CALL to brace for impact, our passengers
kept moving forward. In their hearts and minds, they read-
ied themselves for whatever would follow. In their souls, they
searched for and often found peace. When told to evacuate,
they got their bodies into action—moving, sometimes
painfully slowly, step-by-step down the aisle of the plane,
water rising, still not knowing their fate. Outside, in the
water, on the wing, on a raft, they moved forward, sometimes
against tremendous odds, cold, injury, and fear, toward safety.
And they made it. The first step in their new lives was taken.

To this day they have continued to move forward, learning
the lessons that fateful event had to teach them, becoming
better people, finding deeper truths. And we have the gift
that they have given us: the opportunity to learn and grow.
We invite you to do so now, first with simple exercises that
beckon us into a greater expression of the same qualities that
our passengers have stepped into. We also urge you to join
our online community and website (http://braceforimpact.
hcibooks.com), where these stories continue to unfold.

Working with Qualities:
Exercises for Growing Whole

If, while reading the stories in this book, you've been inspired to do a little inner work yourself, as these passengers have done, here are some exercises to guide you. Each will help you deepen your own relationship to the qualities that have defined this book: faith, gratitude, love, wisdom, healing, and transformation.

Faith

Exercise #1: Living Faith

In the quiet of a moment you carve out for yourself, open the door to your faith, however it lives in you. Invite it in as a feeling, a thought, a sensation, an image. See it, feel it, and know it as the ground of your being. This may be in meditation or prayer, in your own silence, or in nature. The door to your faith will be unique. As you attend to your faith, let it find its form. You may know the form already. It may be your spiritual practice, your religion, your own internal process. Now name it, so that it is strong in you. Complete this paragraph as a journaling exercise. Write as much or as little as you need to, to ground and honor your faith. Revisit this often.

> *"I am living my faith. I . . ."*

Gratitude

Exercise #2: *Thanks for Everything*

Gratitude, they say, makes people healthier and happier. No surprise there, but how easy it is to forget. Take time to write a letter of gratitude. Do this often. This might be a short thank-you note (just like our mothers taught us to do!) or a long letter of deep gratitude. The letter or note might be something you actually send . . . or something you keep.

Write a letter to:

- Someone long gone
- Yourself
- Your church
- The future
- Your husband, wife, parents, children, siblings, cousins, grandparents, aunts, or uncles
- A Sully in your life, somebody who helped steer your course to safety

Who is your Sully: a teacher, a friend, a mentor? Mark had his Colonel Dick, the guy who gave him his first "second chance." You might try a letter to your Sully or that stranger on your plane who helped you out. We all have those kind strangers, too. Maybe just the man down the road who smiled, or the woman who gave you cookies when you were young. Just letting yourself acknowledge these people will open your heart. Writing them a letter will open it even more.

"Dear _____,
I want to thank you for . . . "

Love

Exercise #3: How Do I Love You?

Sometimes it takes a life-altering event to really get how much we love people. But it doesn't need to be that way. Here's an ongoing way to stay connected to your love. Remember the Beatles' famous line, "And in the end, the love you take, is equal to the love you make"?

Make a list on one side of the paper of people you love . . . or like . . . or care about, or any of the many words that describe the experience of open-hearted feelings toward another.

Then go back and ask the question: *How do I show them that I love them?* Write down the answers . . . and if you find the answers don't come easily, you may have to think about that! *If I love her/him/them but I'm not showing it very clearly, I had better fix that.* And that's the last part of the exercise. Make a note about how you *will,* going forward, show your love more fully to the people in your life.

Revisit this list often. Add new people and new ways to express love. One person you might forget to put on that list is yourself. You should be there, too. Have fun with this. Build some more love.

Wisdom

Exercise #4: Resonance

Wisdom comes in all shapes and sizes, and from all sources. Think about that childhood hero you had, or the storybook or cartoon character you liked. What was the wisdom you drew from that figure? We have our classic teachers who have given us wisdom (some better than others!): parents, teachers, mentors, spiritual guides, friends. And we have access to inner wisdom, through our own values, our thinking, our insights, and intuition. Both our body and our feelings offer us wisdom.

Building inner wisdom is as easy as one, two, three:

1) Set the stage for your particular inquiry. Form the question or consideration that you want your own wisdom for. Articulate it as clearly as possible. Writing helps.

2) Think about the question and gather whatever knowledge you already have. Know what you know before looking for more information. Take notes about this, as well. Then wait . . . . a minute, a day, a week. But wait with readiness. For an answer is out there waiting to come to you.

3) Be open to an answer that comes from somewhere other than your thinking. Wait for the "Aha!" that may come through your own intuition. You may suddenly see something in the world that gives you insight. Your feelings or body may guide you to the next level. You will know it because it will resonate. It will feel right; there will be no judgment, no "should." It will be a breath of fresh air. Trust that knowing!

Healing

Exercise #5: Better and Better

We can't make healing happen, but we can set the stage for healing. Like the cast on a broken bone, the support we've put in place helps a very natural process of healing. And we all need healing, whether it is from our physical, emotional, or spiritual wounds and suffering. Healing, in the physical world, is not even about cure, though we would always like it to be when someone we love is ill. Healing may, instead, be about wholeness, even in the face of difficulty, even in the face of death. Healing, then, requires our cooperation and our intention: the intention to be better and better, every day and in every way. Slowly but surely.

Think about the timeline of your life, past . . . present . . . future.

Ask these questions, and think about/feel about them, and write your answers:

How have I grown more whole since I was a child?

What have I learned over my life that I now use to be a better person?

What is facing me in my present life that has something to teach me?

Am I attending to that? Am I learning the lessons?

As I move into my future, what does a *more whole* me look like?

How can I give life to that better me that I want to become?

Transformation

Exercise #6: Conscious Evolution

Transformation is the moment-to-moment experience of change that every living thing experiences. We may grow an inch and not even notice, or we may work hard to change a behavior or attitude. Being conscious of ourselves in the process of growth and change helps facilitate that change. We will evolve with or without our own help, but if we help, our evolution will be a more powerful movement. Sometimes this is nearly impossible to do. Sometimes we are fully aware and in the flow of our own change. Bringing attention to bear will simply move our own inevitable transformation along toward the values that are most important to us. This is awakening to purpose.

We all know about the five-year plan, the New Year's resolutions, the lists, the shoulds coming from inside us and from outside. Try a different approach. Work with this idea in drawing, writing, moving, conversation, and life every day.

In my heart of hearts, I want . . .

In my heart of hearts, I know . . .

In my heart of hearts, I care about . . .

In my heart of hearts, I am . . .

In my heart of hearts, my life . . .

Get to know your heart of hearts, the voice of your soul, the call of Self. Let this inner knowing guide your transformation.

Join Us!

Our online community (http://braceforimpact.hcibooks.com) is a part of the work of this book. Our twenty-five passengers and first responders are there, with an active presence as their stories continue to unfold. Videos of some of their talks, appearances, and news stories are available for you to view. You also can get more directly involved. As readers you can share your thoughts and feelings and be in touch with the passengers, first responders, and the authors. We will share new exercises for you to try, to keep us all working toward wholeness.

We've also provided a forum for you to contribute your own story that tells of an impactful event in your life. Visit the site for guidelines. We hope you will take the time to share your story. Each of us has a story to tell, and on this site we want to build a world of hope, to create new life, to face the "airplane crash" that each of us has had in one way or another. Transformation awaits us all.

Good-bye for Now

Thank you for journeying with us through the lives of some extraordinary people and their extraordinary journey. We are all travelers in our own way, each moving through a lifetime, the best way we know how. The stories we have heard of a near-death experience, a miracle, and the unfolding of lives over time have much to teach us. Each of us is on this same journey, one way or another. And for each step taken, there is a ripple effect. Our passengers went home to people who loved them, and they too have stories to tell. Total strangers, moved by this event, have shown up, also with stories to tell. And beyond that, in the unfolding of a life—their lives, our lives, all lives—there is the future that will find us learning new lessons. We will take our inspiration into the world and change the world (even a little).

So many lessons to take away from our travelers: Barry Leonard, Bill Elkin, Lucille Palmer and Diane Higgins, Warren Holland, Darren Beck, Michele Davis, Mark Hood, Scott Koen, Brad Wentzell, Maryann Bruce, Matt Kane, Don Norton, Debbie Ramsey, Billy Campbell, Ray Basri, Vicki Barnhardt, Glenn Carlson, Bill Zuhoski, Beth McHugh, Dave Sanderson, Hilda Roque-Dieguez, Gerry McNamara, Claudette Mason, Jerry Shanko. They have been our guides, and we thank them dearly.